HOW COME IT'S CALLED THAT?

GEOGRAPHY OF THE BIG BEND REGION

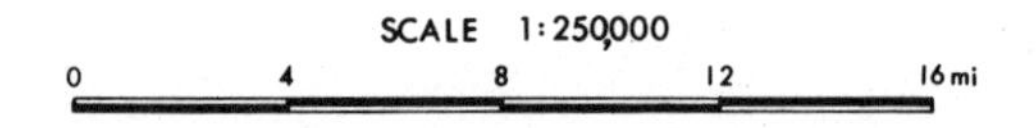

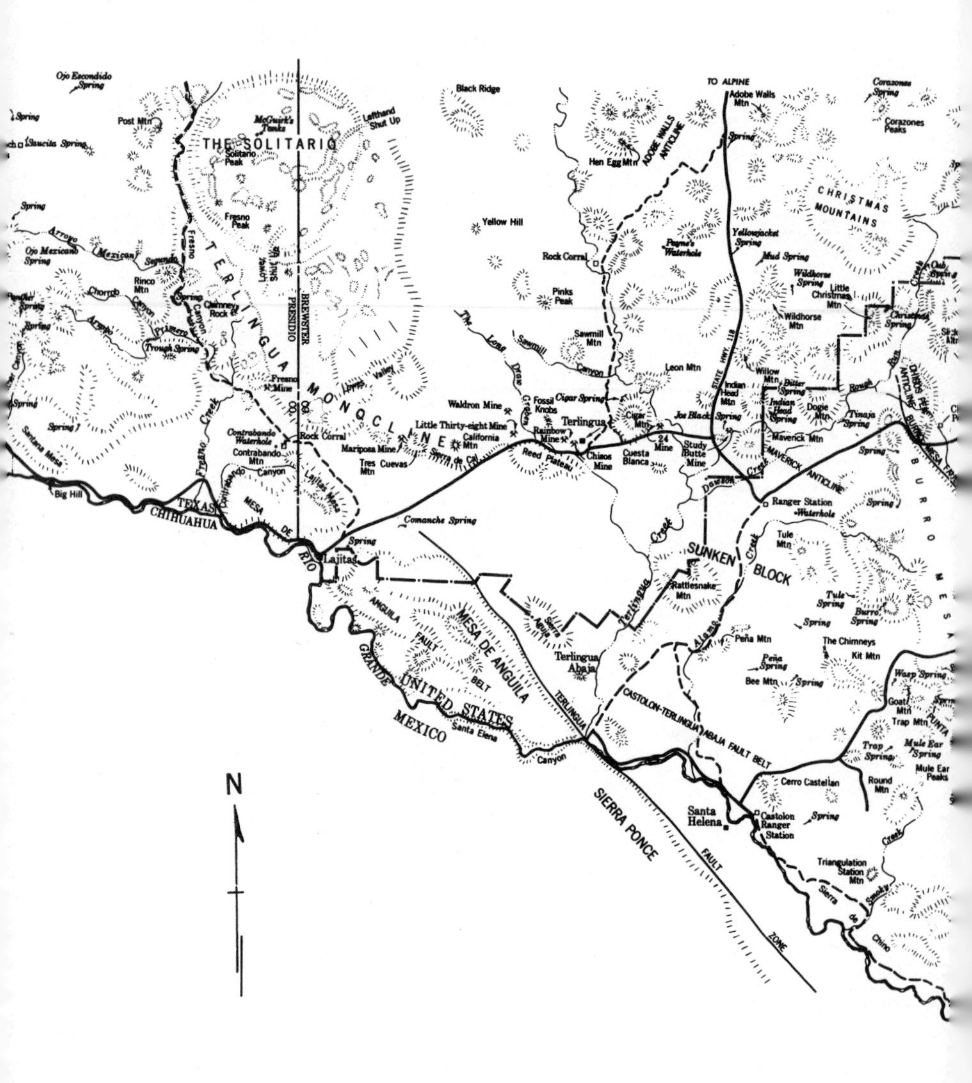

Map Courtesy of The University of Texas Bureau of Economic Geology

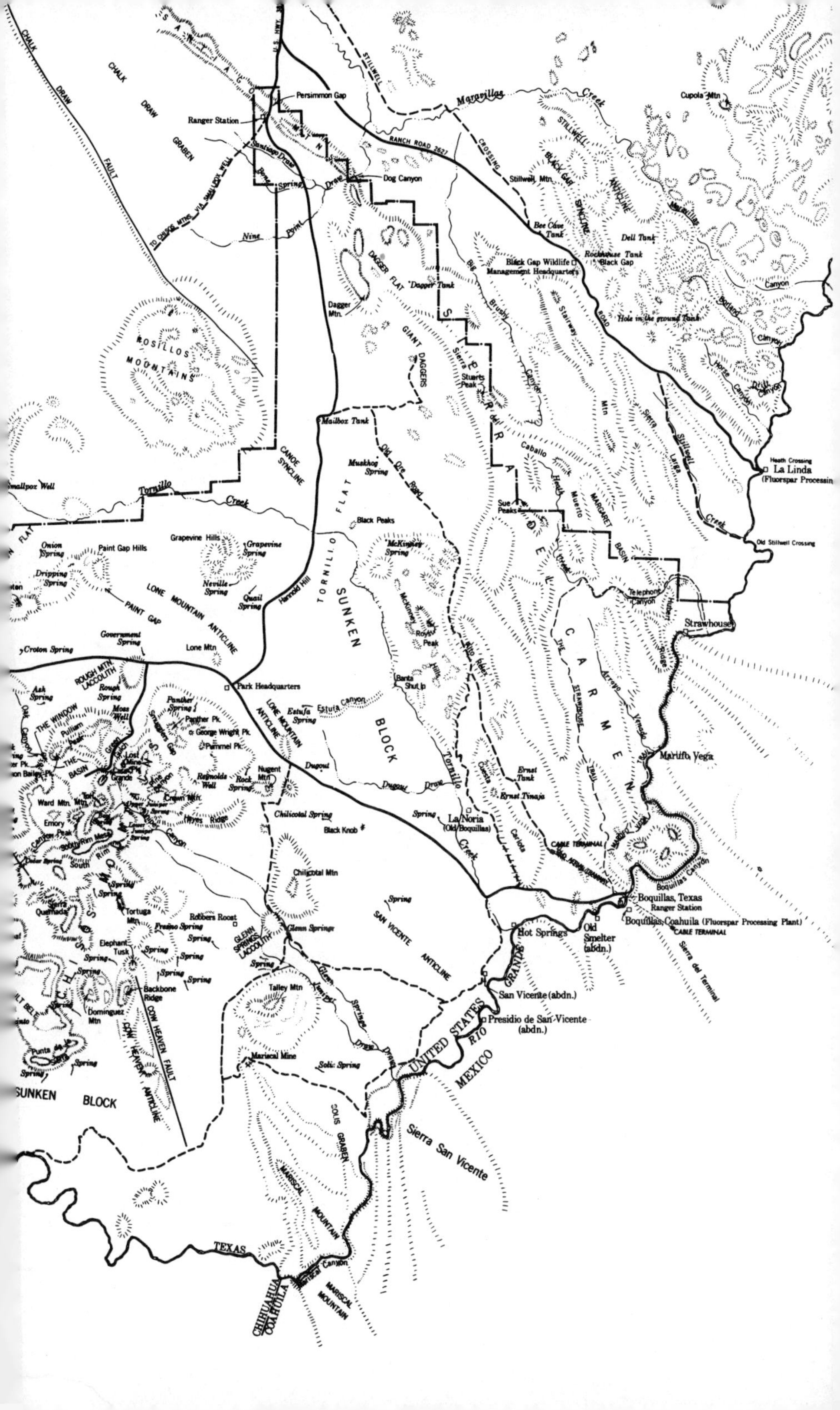

Persimmon Gap
Ranger Station
Dog Canyon
CHALK DRAW GRABEN
CHALK DRAW FAULT
RANCH ROAD 2627
Maravillas Creek
Cupola Mtn
Stillwell Mtn
Bee Cave Tank
Dell Tank
Rockhouse Tank
Black Gap
Black Gap Wildlife Management Headquarters
Dagger Tank
Dagger Mtn.
DAGGER FLAT
GIANT DAGGERS
ROSILLOS MOUNTAINS
Nine Point
Stuarts Peak
Hole in the ground Tank
Heath Crossing
La Linda (Fluorspar Processing)
Old Stillwell Crossing
Mailbox Tank
Muskhog Spring
Old Ore Road
CANOE SYNCLINE
Smallpox Well
Tornillo Creek
Black Peaks
Sue Peaks
MARGARET BASIN
Grapevine Hills
Grapevine Spring
Paint Gap Hills
Onion Spring
Dripping Spring
McKinney Spring
Neville Spring
Quail Spring
LONE MOUNTAIN ANTICLINE
PAINT GAP
Harrold Hill
TORNILLO FLAT
SUNKEN BLOCK
Telephone Canyon
Strawhouse
Roys Peak
Government Spring
Lone Mtn
Croton Spring
ROUGH MTN. LACCOLITH
Park Headquarters
Banta Shut In
CARMEN
Estufa Spring
Estufa Canyon
Ash Spring
Rough Spring
THE WINDOW
Panther Pk.
George Wright Pk.
Pummel Pk.
Mariscal Vega
Lost Mine Pk.
Casa Grande
Nugent Mtn
Rock Spring
Reynolds Well
Dugout
Dugout Draw
Ernst Tank
Ernst Tinaja
Ward Mtn.
Emory Peak
Crown Mtn.
Hayes Ridge
Chilicotal Spring
Black Knob
La Noria (Old Boquillas)
CABLE TERMINAL
Boquillas Canyon
Chilicotal Mtn
Boquillas, Texas
Ranger Station
Boquillas, Coahuila (Fluorspar Processing Plant)
CABLE TERMINAL
Sierra Quemada
Tortuga Mtn
Robbers Roost
Fresno Spring
Glenn Springs
GLENN SPRINGS LACCOLITH
SAN VICENTE ANTICLINE
Hot Springs
Old Smelter (abdn.)
Sierra del Carmen
Elephant Tusk
Backbone Ridge
Dominguez Mtn
COW HEAVEN FAULT
COW HEAVEN ANTICLINE
Talley Mtn
San Vicente (abdn.)
Presidio de San Vicente (abdn.)
UNITED STATES
RIO GRANDE
MEXICO
Punta de la Sierra
Mariscal Mine
Solis Spring
SUNKEN BLOCK
SOLIS GRABEN
Sierra San Vicente
MARISCAL MOUNTAIN
TEXAS
Mariscal Canyon
CHIHUAHUA
COAHUILA

How Come

It's Called

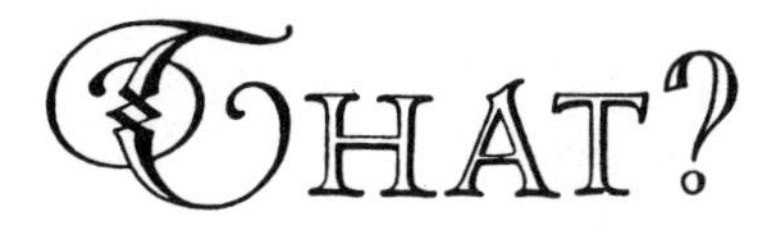

Place Names in the Big Bend Country

by Virginia Madison

&

Hallie Stillwell

Iron Mountain Press

Marathon, Texas

1997

Iron Mountain Press printings:
May, 1997 - 8000 copies

ISBN 0-9657985-0-X

Printed and Bound by:
Hart Graphics
Austin, Texas

Iron Mountain Press
P.O. Box 325
Marathon, Texas 79842

Cover Photo: Santa Elena Canyon. National Park Service.

DEDICATION

T*O THE PIONEERS* whose names, experiences and sayings have given names to places in the Big Bend Country and to those early mapmakers whose work located on maps the features bearing those names.

ACKNOWLEDGMENTS

WE SHOULD LIKE to express our appreciation to all those Big Benders who hunted up family records, sent us clippings from old newspaper files, wrote us letters about experiences which served as background for place names and told us stories of family names which were affixed to mountains, canyons or trails. Each contribution helped preserve another page of regional history.

We are deeply indebted to the late Arthur A. Stiles for his report on "How the Mountains Were Named" which was written after he completed his topographic map of the Big Bend country in 1903. Personal interviews with Mr. and Mrs. Stiles brought to light much new information about place names in the region—information which Mr. Stiles was able to substantiate with written records and maps.

For his account of the surveyors' experiences while working with Mr. Stiles in the Big Bend, we wish to thank Stuart T. Penick of La Grange, Texas.

In interviews with the late Captain E. E. Townsend, known as the father of Big Bend National Park, we learned many stories about place names in the park area and we wish to acknowledge his assistance.

The late Henry T. Fletcher of Marfa, Texas, and the late Judge O. W. Williams of Fort Stockton, Texas, spent much time searching out the stories behind the place names in the Trans-Pecos. Their accounts as published in the Alpine *Avalanche* and privately printed bulletins were invaluable to us in writing this book.

For stories about the naming of places along the Southern Pacific Railroad, we are indebted to the late W. R. Mann who was Assistant Superintendent of the Southern Pacific for years.

We should like to express our appreciation to Dr. Ross A. Maxwell, first Superintendent of Big Bend National Park and now of the University of Texas, and Dr. Meredith F. Burrill, Director of the U.S. Board on Geographic Names, Washington, D.C. for their assistance and cooperation.

For new information on the naming of the Chisos Mountains, we wish to thank Lic. Antonio Fernandez del Castillo, Secretary and Treasurer of the National Academy of History and Geography, Mexico City; Dr. Elton Miles, Sul Ross State College, Alpine, Texas, and Dr. Frederick J. Dockstader, Assistant Director of the Museum of the American Indian, New York City.

We are indebted to the following for their contributions to this volume or their cooperation on the research: Conrad L. Wirth, Director of the National Park Service; Douglas McKay, former Secretary of the Interior; George W. Miller, Superintendent of Big Bend National Park; Lemuel A. Garrison, Superintendent of Yellowstone National Park and a former superintendent of Big Bend National Park; C. M. Meadows, Sr., San Angelo, Texas; Presley Bryant, Ft. Worth, Texas; Barry Scobee of Fort Davis, Texas; Mrs. W. Sumner Halcomb, Sam Woolford, Mrs. I. L. Kleinman and Col. H. M. Henderson of San Antonio, Texas; Frank D. Quinn, former Chairman of Texas State Parks Board, Austin, Texas; Dr. Benjamin F. Berkeley, Dr. Horace W. Morelock, W. D. Burcham, Captain C. D. Wood, Gene Cartledge, Mr. and Mrs. J. E. Casner, Charles Hunter, Glenn Burgess, Gus Rountree, Tom Carney, R. N. Pulliam, and Jim Walker, all of Alpine, Texas; Bob Cartledge of Castolon; Mrs. L. C. Brite, Mrs. Oren Bunton, Mrs. John Humphris and Wayne Cartledge of Marfa, Texas; T. B. Henderson and J. J. Roberts of Marathon, Texas; Mrs. Esther Russell Devine, Laredo, Texas; and Mrs. Maggie Smith of Boquillas, Mexico.

For taking the time to read and criticize the manuscript, we say, "Muchas gracias" to Mrs. Oren Bunton, W. D. Burcham and John W. Gillett, all of whom know the Big Bend country well and have been associated with every phase of its development.

Virginia Madison
Hallie Stillwell

CONTENTS

INTRODUCTION

ROAD MAPS and guidebooks a-plenty have been worked out by experts at watching sign-posts and mile-markers to lead you through the trails and canyons and up the mountains of the Big Bend country, so we have in no way attempted to chart your course. However if any of your explorations in the region cause you to wonder at the peculiar-sounding name attached to some remote place, or if there seems to be no logic whatsoever in the name of a spring, mountain or canyon, drag out this little volume and find out how come it's called that.

If there are several versions to the story of how a place was named we have given all the versions, but if you find something you don't believe, remember that this is how we heard it, for all the stories came from the people. And you will miss the most important commodity the Big Bend has to offer if you don't get to know the people.

In a region where the people are individualists, it is impossible to get all the good stories between the covers of one book, for there are just as many good yarns as there are individuals. If you hear a story about the naming of some landmark which we did not include, jot it down, for it will give you a bright peg upon which to hang your memory of that place.

Chapter 1

WHAT'S IN A NAME? —HISTORY AND HAPPENINGS

O*NCE* a Brewster County resident, who had been in the region some forty-odd years, inquired of an old cowman who had spent seventy years in the Big Bend, "Roy, can you tell me why in tarnation they call that break between the Santiago Mountains and the Dead Horse 'Dog Canyon?' "

"Sure, I can tell you how come it's called that." And out came the tale in a very few words. "Years ago when one of the early settlers was going through that particular canyon, he found a wagon and ox-team with a dog guarding them. There was no trace of the owner. From then on it was called 'Dog Canyon.' " On the earliest maps this canyon is called *Cañon del Perro*—Spanish for Dog Canyon.

Sometimes there is more to a name than meets the eye, and only those who were there when the christening took place can tell it straight. It's a dead cinch that when the old-timers were naming certain places in the Big Bend Country in Texas and telling tales of incidents which happened at those places, they didn't expect to have to explain how come they called them that, nor did they know that those tales would live through the years, being told and retold until they became place names and part of the region's history. Those with the wildest imaginations never dreamed that tourists, scientists, and students would be gallivanting around on that wild, thorn-incubating frontier which early mapmakers called the Bad Lands of Texas. And from those early mapmakers come the most authentic stories of how many of the places were named.

The Big Bend Country was almost a nameless land when the topographical engineers began to map the region in 1902 and 1903. Of course a few names were fixed in the region—some were supplied by the early Indians, a few had been used as guideposts for exploring Spaniards and a few more had been added by the United States Boundary Commission between 1848 and 1852. Others had appeared on the maps of the routes of the camel caravans in 1859 and 1860, especially names of waterholes and springs, for water was the important factor in the camel experiments. Some of those names have been changed now, but others have remained to be passed on by the U. S. Board on Geographic Names and we hope they will become permanently fixed in history with the publication of the true story of *How Come It's Called That.*

In the minds of most researchers there is always that element of doubt as to how a physiographical or topographical feature came by its name unless they can arrive at the original source. With the exception of those first few names recorded in our early Texas history or the Spanish history of the Big Bend Country, we are fortunate to have the personal statements from those two engineers who mapped and named many of the features in the Big Bend back in 1902 and 1903. And those names were not just tacked onto the places, but they were put on the map with the will and consent of the people who lived in the region at that time and by those who had enough interest in such matters to attend the meeting at which the naming took place.

During the summer of 1956, we met and had a long conference with Mr. and Mrs. Arthur A. Stiles. Mr. Stiles was in charge of the party which made the topographical survey of the Big Bend in 1902-03. He gave us the name of the young man who worked with him then—Stuart T. Penick. Mr. Stiles and Mr. Penick both wrote down their experiences on that assignment and gave us the original records of how those names happened to be as they are. Few writers ever have the good fortune and the opportunity for such conferences. Here, fifty-five years after those names were added to the map of the Big Bend Country, the two engineers who mapped the region draw on memory and recorded materials to tell their story of the place names and how come they were called that.

The following is an exact copy of the report written by Arthur A. Stiles:

HOW THE MOUNTAINS WERE NAMED

This was in the Big Bend Country of Texas where the glistening Rio Grande loops around the Chisos Mountains.

After two years of hard and exacting topographic work for the United States Geological Survey, we were finishing this job of mapping. With our all but worn out saddle horses and pack mules, we were returning over the range to our headquarters at Boquillas, Texas.

Our headquarters consisted of three snow-white Army tents glistening in the sunlight.

Boquillas consisted of an adobe store house with living quarters nearby. The store served as a post office, a saloon and a Justice of the Peace Court.

Boquillas was not a crowded place. The Southern Pacific Railroad depot was one-hundred and twenty miles out of town. Homes on the ranches were estimated to be 25 to 60 miles apart.

But the people were much interested in our mapping of their country. Their main fear was that the maps that we were finishing might come out with only one name, the name, Boquillas.

But Mr. Ernst, the storekeeper and Justice of the Peace promptly declared: "We will name all of these places: thereupon he called a jury to meet upon the subject at Boquillas.[1]

---

1. In the conference with Mr. Stiles, he said that riders were sent out in every direction to tell people of the meeting to be held to consider place names. The time and place were given and the people were given a thirty-day notice. On the day of the meeting they came riding in from all directions!

The jury came on horseback from many distances and directions; and seemed delighted to serve.

I was invited to attend this meeting, and did so, using our topographic maps from which to determine the correct positions of the features in question.

On the day of the meeting of Mr. Ernst's jury, we all gathered at noon in my office tent upon which was hoisted the United States Flag. I had promised to serve dinner to the gathering in my tent. I cooked the dinner myself and served it. It consisted of roast venison, fried quail, baked sweet potatoes, corn pudding, wild honey, and coffee.

After dinner Mr. Ernst called his jury together and acted as foreman. Mr. McNeeley was selected secretary.

The geographic names were then presented and carefully examined. Each prominent feature of the country was given a name.

Each member of the jury was complimented by having a topographic feature for a namesake. The jury was temporarily dismissed subject to recall by Mr. Ernst who was also selected general custodian of records.

When it came to naming all of the places, it developed that there were barely enough people living in the country to furnish names for all the places; and Mr. Ernst had to act independently.

He called an unnamed range of mountains to the west the Stiles Mountains. A high peak in this same range, he called Sue Peaks for my sweetheart who is now my wife. A striking topographic feature he named Margaret Basin in honor of my mother.

Mr. McNeeley wrote the record.

A list of topographic names was to go far out across the desert to County Judge Turney and by his order would become part of the records of Brewster County, Texas.

Thus the meeting ended.

The meeting in my tent at Boquillas, Texas took place late in December in 1903.

I wrote this record in February, 1908.

The record was never published.

Respectfully,

Arthur A. Stiles,
Austin, Texas

One of the most rewarding items of information to come from the meeting with Mr. Stiles was the authentic story of how Sue Peaks and Margaret Basin came by their names. For years both writers of this book heard varying stories from different sources. Time and again we were asked if we could find out where those names came from. We did find out and had the privilege to talk with the charming and vivacious lady for whom Sue Peaks was named—Mrs. Arthur A. Stiles herself—Susie, as her husband calls her. They were married soon after his assignment in the Big Bend was finished and his superior gave him an assignment in California so they could go to the Portland, Oregon, Exposition for their honeymoon.

In the Big Bend Country, Sue Peaks will always remind those who see them and know their story that this land of romance was first mapped by a young engineer, the first graduate of the Texas University Engineering Department, who enjoyed his lonely assignment on the Texas-Mexican Border because his lovely bride-to-be waited in Austin, Texas, until he finished his job and could return for their wedding. Theirs is a beautiful love story and it is fitting that a beautiful feature of the romantic Big Bend should remind us of it.

Mr. Ernst, who was foreman of the jury on place names, was the one to suggest that Margaret Basin be named for the mother of the young engineer. We hope this authentic story lays to rest any further speculation and fabrication about how come Sue Peaks and Margaret Basin are named what they are.

We were told by Mr. Stiles that Stuart T. Penick, now living at La Grange, Texas, has the best memory for names of any person he knows. In answer to our query, Mr. Penick wrote:

> —*We count Mr. and Mrs. Stiles among our very best friends. In fact, I give Mr. Stiles credit for whatever success I may have attained as a Topographic Engineer, for it was under his tutelage for two years that I learned the art. Mr. Stiles was one of the best topographers that the U. S. Geological Survey ever had, and I was fortunate in having had him to instruct me in topographic surveying.*[2] *However, I am afraid that my good friend has exaggerated my capacity for remembering names.*
>
> *It was by accident that I joined Mr. Stiles' camp in the Big Bend Country in the summer of 1902. I was working my way through the University of Texas, when at the close of school in June of my second year there, Dr. Wm. B. Phillips, professor of Mineralogy, offered to take me to the Chisos Mountains where he was going to study the geology in that vicinity. I got a thrill before I got near the Big Bend Country, for the train stopped at Langtry, and we saw and talked with Roy Bean (Law West of the Pecos). Crossing the Pecos High Bridge was another thrill for a country boy on his first trip away*

2. "Since my day and preceding Dr. J. A. Udden, a splendid topographic map of the Big Bend region was made by Arthur A. Stiles, one of the best topographers of the United States Geological Survey. Stiles was an Austin boy of whose skill in map-making line all Texans should be justly proud. A study of this map should be the first step by anyone today who wishes to understand the Big Bend region." Dr. Robert T. Hill, "Musings and Memories of the Big Bend. When it Was the Bloody Bend and Other Things," *The Dallas Morning News,* Oct. 24, 1937.

from home. Upon reaching Marfa, Dr. Phillips purchased a light wagon and team, hired a Mexican as a combination teamster and cook, and we proceeded 90 miles south to the Terlingua Mines. Mr. Stiles was in charge of a U. S. Geological Survey party and was camped a short distance from the mines. The party was just finishing a special Mineral Survey, of which Dr. Phillips was the director. We spent several days with Mr. Stiles and then proceeded southeastward to the foot hills of the Chisos Mountains, where we struck camp.

In a few days a messenger came from Mr. Stiles saying that his teamster had quit and asked Dr. Phillips if I could come and act as teamster until he could get someone for the job. Dr. Phillips left it up to me, assuring me that it would not inconvenience him if I wanted to go back and help Mr. Stiles out, so I returned and acted as teamster for the camp. Shortly afterward, one of the instrument men was transferred and Mr. Stiles was instructed to break in a new man. Several young fellows were tried out for the place, but none of them made the grade. I did not apply for a trial, for I was not an engineering student. In the meantime, Dr. Phillips suggested that I be given a trial. After some instruction from Mr. Stiles in the use of a Plane table, I was assigned a small area to make a contour map of, and when it was completed, it was submitted to Mr. Stiles for inspection. In some way I made the grade, and was hired as an instrument man in the U. S. Geological Survey.

The special area of the Terlingua Mine having been completed we started mapping the remainder of the 30′ Quadrangle and worked eastward, moving camp as we went and by the fall of 1903 we reached Ernst's store which was near the head of Boquillas Canyon and was as far down the Rio

Grande as it was possible to travel with a wagon. From there eastward the going was very hard, even on horseback. That area is called the Boquillas and is a series of box canyons emptying into the Rio Grande. I believe it is the most difficult country that I have ever traversed.

In 1902, the Big Bend was pretty wild country. The stage brought mail and passengers to Terlingua once a week from Marfa and that was the only outside connection there was. There were temporary cow camps in the area where the spring and fall roundups were made, but most of the ranches were closer to the railroad towns of Marfa, Marathon, and Alpine and only a few cowboys were in the area between roundups. Often for days and weeks we would see no one except those in our camp. The area at that time was a favorite hangout for cattle rustlers. It was easy to run cattle from one side of the Rio Grande to the other. Texas Rangers were scarce and they didn't get to that part of the country very often. We followed the custom of the time and carried sixshooters on our hip and a 30-30 in the scabbard on our saddles, but for shooting game, which was very plentiful, and for sport. We gave the rustlers a wide berth. We sent to Sears and had ammunition sent out by the case, for we used a lot of it to keep in practice.

I remember the Stillwell Ranch, but I am not sure about the naming of Dead Horse Mountains. ——We could well have applied that name to some of the limestone ridges we had to cross in the Boquillas Country, where we had to make many pack trips, and some of them were so long, hard and dry, that on several occasions a pack animal would give out and be unable to make it through to the watering place.

We finished the work in the Big Bend Country in

December, 1903, disbanded camp, and Mr. Stiles went to the Washington office and I returned to the University of Texas to take some special courses in topographic drawing and surveying.

Practically all of my work with the Geological Survey was in the Rocky Mountains Section, for, thanks to Mr. Stiles' expert training, I became an expert in mapping rough terrain, handling a pack outfit, and I was called the "Rocky Mountain Goat" of the Survey. I traveled over the greater part of the Continental Divide from southern Arizona to northern Montana with a pack outfit.

Having reached the retirement age in March, 1940, I was retired at that time from the United States Geological Survey after thirty-eight years of service.[3] *The first eighteen months of that period spent in the Big Bend Country seem to stand out more vividly than any other period during those thirty-eight years.*

If you can use any of this account, you are welcome to do so.

Sincerely,

Stuart T. Penick

These two men told us that they always used the local names for places if there were any names in use at that time, and in many cases they were able to tell us why certain names were applied to the regional features. They took their work seriously and today are interested in seeing that only accurate information is attributed to them.

There are Indian, Spanish, and American legends about

3. During World War II, when engineers became scarce, Mr. Penick helped map several cantonments and ammunition plants, and when that was done, he again retired. Later a geophysical survey ran short of engineers and asked him to help out. In 1947, when the boys began coming out of the Army, he retired for the third time and that is his status at present.

the naming of some of the places. The preponderance of Spanish names shows the Spanish influence in the region. Many mountains, springs and canyons are named for the men who first settled there. Others are named for their similarity to familiar objects such as tusks, eggs, boots and saddles. Such names were used because there were not enough people living in the region to give persons' names to all the features. Some places are named for incidents which happened there and years of reference to such incidents christened the places and the names stuck, although "how come it's called that" has been forgotten by all but a few old-timers. Take for instance the battle of Adobe Walls. As long as two or more of those who took part in that episode were living, they loved nothing better than recalling the circumstances of that fight. This battle should not be confused with the one by the same name which took place in the Panhandle of Texas where Quanah and his braves made an attack on an organized company of white buffalo hunters in 1874.

The adobe walls in the Big Bend were erected as the walls of the G-4 ranch house back in 1886 but were never finished. A seep spring had been dug out on the lower side of the ridge, making an excavation which held about four barrels of water. The G-4 outfit was camped on the upper side of the ridge with the adobe walls between them and the spring. Lechuguillas and many types of cacti grew around the campsite. One night two Texas Rangers rode into camp and bedded down with the cowboys. Some think that they were on the lookout for Jim Davenport who had killed old man Hereford, but others say that they had gotten word of the shooting and just happened to be in camp when Jim tried to slip in to contact his brother, Jeff, who was working for the G-4.

Anyway, that night they placed their bed rolls near that of Jeff Davenport. Sometime in the night Jim rode into camp, dog-tired and thirsty. He stopped to get a drink at the bucket which hung under the arbor in front of the camp. He called to his brother. The Rangers got the drop on him and ordered him to put up his hands. Jim started shooting instead. The

Rangers managed to get behind a wagon and returned the fire. Davenport headed for the brush. The frightened cowboys jumped up and scattered like quail. One long-legged *vaquero* headed for the corral with a shorter member of the outfit running behind him, beseeching him to tell what the shooting was all about. Two others sleeping near each other grabbed hands and tore out barefooted through the lechuguilla and mesquite thorns, holding hands like two schoolboys. Another scared cowboy was facing the adobe walls when he jumped up and he said he was running so damn fast that he ran entirely around them and squatted down against the wall on the side next to the shooting.

Jim escaped and followed the trail which led to the spring where he drank and worked his way over the hill where he hid and watched the Rangers depart next morning. Then he came into camp where he was among friends. He ate, had his wounds dressed, and borrowed a fresh horse to make a getaway.

All the old-timers who were there the night of the battle of Adobe Walls in the Big Bend have gone on now, but as long as they lived they enjoyed preening their stories to ridicule the antics of a friend who ran like a scared jackrabbit when he awoke to find his camp turned into bedlam with bullets kicking gravel into his face.

Many place names in the Big Bend are appropriately descriptive of the landmarks which they identify, while others are remembered by something which happened there. Take Robber's Roost. Down in the Chisos Mountains the robbers have long ago departed, but not many years ago the late Pete Crawford, Texas Ranger, told about two young fellows from an Eastern state who arrived in the Big Bend of Texas with revolvers and adventurous intentions. Before reaching Alpine, where the road drops down into the Big Bend, they held up a motorist and relieved him of his cash and car. Pete went after them and shortly thereafter they were in jail in Alpine. Pete was always interested in finding out why bandits become bandits so he asked, "Why did you boys come to this part of the country?" "Well," answered one of the would-be gunmen, "we had a map of the Big Bend Country and saw that it had a small population. Then we saw the place marked Robber's Roost and decided to come out here and join the gang." In Presidio County there is another place by the name of Robber's Roost which is remembered by old-timers as the place where hundreds of cattle met their deaths in a strange stampede.[4]

---

4. Virginia Madison, *The Big Bend Country*, U.N.M. Press, Albuquerque, N.M., 1955, pp. 138-39.

Chapter 2

THE BIG BEND NATIONAL PARK

MOST PEOPLE visit the Big Bend Country for the express purpose of seeing the Big Bend National Park and immediately wonder how come it's called that. The antics of the Rio Grande gave the region its name and the park established within that region naturally bears the same name. So far as we are able to determine, the first person actually to refer to this spectacular region as the Big Bend Country was Lt. W. H. C. Whiting who conducted in 1840 a reconnaissance from San Antonio to El Paso for the Army Engineers. In his journal dated March 12 at Escondido Springs and referring to the Comanche War Trail he wrote: "This trail strikes southwest for a few miles and then by south course crosses the Rio Grande in the Big Bend." And, at Fort Leaton March 25—"The whole of the neighboring region of the Big Bend requires thorough reconnaissance."[1]

Perhaps the most important name in the whole region is the Rio Grande (Spanish words for Great River). Not only does the big bend in its journey to the sea give a name to the region within the boundaries of its bend, but it plays an important role in the lives of the people living within reach of its influence. Paul Horgan said of this river, "The main physical circumstances of the Rio Grande are timeless. They assume meaning only in terms of people who came to the river."[2]

---

1. Cited by Dr. Elton Miles, Sul Ross College, from *Exploring Southwest Trails 1846-1854,* Vol. VII (R. P. Bieber, ed.), Arthur H. Clark Co., Glendale, Cal., 1938, pp. 256-88.

2. Paul Horgan, *Great River,* Vol. 1, Rinehart & Co., New York, 1954, p. 7.

Beginning in Colorado, the river cuts its way southward to the present site of El Paso and there veers to the southeast as if reaching straight for the Gulf of Mexico, but about one hundred miles below El Paso, at the adobe village of Porvenir, the stream changes its course and swings back to the south, bending itself around almost seven million acres of canyon, mountain, and desert. Cradling these geological phenomena in its mighty elbow, the river resumes its southeasterly course, after its junction with San Francisco Creek, to deposit the waste from its excavations into the Gulf of Mexico. In 1882 this strange isolated land, bounded on two sides by the Rio Grande, was separated from the rest of the Trans-Pecos by the Southern Pacific Railroad, then being built from San Antonio to El Paso. The railroad took a short cut by following a straight line across the Big Bend instead of following the course of the river. It was then that this big chunk of Texas north of the border and south of the tracks began to develop its own personality.

A few citizens who knew something of the scenic wonders of the Big Bend Country goaded those in a position to do something about it into making a trip to the region to see for themselves what was down there. As a result, the National Park Service threw a federal fence around about three-quarters of a million acres of this region where it is now being preserved for everybody to enjoy. In the deepest pocket of the river's bend lies the Big Bend National Park.

Our present Director of National Parks, Mr. Conrad Wirth, was one of the park officials who went to investigate the reports of a scenic and unspoiled wonderland which should be protected. He liked what he saw and turned his convictions into actions, working with those on the immediate scene until the job was finished. The area Mr. Wirth went to see in 1934 was officially established as a park on June 12, 1944, and on July 5, 1944, it was opened by the first superintendent, Dr. Ross A. Maxwell. Thereafter, the formal dedication was planned and postponed a number of times. Conditions immediately following World War II made the dedication impossible. Then the cold war, the Korean War and other crises halted Dedication Day. Finally on November 19, 1955, the lead editorial of the Fort Worth *Star-Telegram* stated: "That the event is now taking place is evidence in itself of an atmosphere more nearly approaching peace than the world has been accustomed to in recent years."

Weeks before Dedication Day rolled around, the Big Bend National Park Development Committee, headed by Paul Forchheimer, laid plans for an event which has now passed into the history of the Big Bend National Park.

At 11:30 on the morning of November 21, 1955, over a thousand guests assembled in Nature's great amphitheater, the Basin, to hear this vast, brilliant land dedicated as our twenty-seventh national park.

A lot of work, planning and legislation goes into the creation and protection of these areas of great natural resources and beauty. Millions of people each year visit our national parks and enjoy scenery which would have been overrun by industry and spoiled by thoughtlessness were it not for the public-minded conservationists who want future generations to see what early Americans saw when they first explored this great land of ours. So the far-flung mesh of the net of our national park system makes it possible for every tourist to see little segments of almost every section of our beautiful America in their natural integrity.

On this day of dedication, which had been so long anticipated, the weather co-operated with the citizens to make it a perfect day in the Big Bend. As the Sul Ross College Lobo Band, arrayed in vivid uniforms of scarlet and gray, presented a concert, the warm sun shone down from a cloudless sky on the flag-draped speaker's stand which was crowded with honored guests.

Congressman J. T. Rutherford, as master of ceremonies, kept the program moving along at a fast clip as cameras clicked and rolled to record for all time that colorful event being witnessed by only a representative few. Visitors were welcomed by Park Superintendent George W. Miller; and the president of the Park Development Committee, Paul

Forchheimer, spoke to the assembled guests in both English and Spanish as a courtesy to the Mexican officials and guests present. After the band played *Himno Nacional,* the Mexican National Anthem, Governor Jesús Lozoya Solis of Chihuahua; Enrique Ballesteros, Mexican consul general from El Paso; Dr. Alfredo Madrigal of Chihuahua; and Juan Estrada, Mayor of Ciudad Acuna, were introduced. Then the honored guests, those men and women who had worked toward the culmination of this great project for many years, were introduced. Special tribute was paid to the late Captain E. E. Townsend, known as the father of the Big Bend National Park, and to the late Amon G. Carter, Sr., fondly referred to as Mr. Texas, the man who supported every phase of the Park's development. Then Secretary of the Interior Douglas McKay spoke to the assembled guests:

DEDICATION SPEECH

This is a proud and memorable occasion.

We have gathered in this setting of wild and majestic natural beauty to dedicate for the benefit and enjoyment of all the people for all time the Big Bend National Park.

I share with all of you a profound sorrow that we could not be joined on this happy occasion by that great son of Texas and noble American, Dwight D. Eisenhower.

I know you rejoice with me, however, in the progress he has made toward full recovery.

The dedication of this, the seventh largest of all our 28 national parks, is, indeed, a happy event in the administration of President Eisenhower. Not alone because of his very deep and sincere appreciation of the priceless values of our national parks, nor because the Big Bend is in his native state.

More significant is the fact that this park was conceived as a symbol of international peace.

It was formally established on June 12, 1944, while our soldiers were fighting to establish a beachhead in France.

When peace finally came after that terrible war, it proved

only temporary. Plans for this dedication ceremony had to be shelved while sons of Texas joined other American boys on the bloody battlefields of Korea.

Today the hopes for lasting peace have been raised for peoples throughout the world to the highest point they have been in a decade. People of all nations seem now to look more to their hearts than to their armed might in developing plans for a peaceful world. It is altogether fitting then, that in this era of heartfelt hope, we should dedicate this great gift from the people of Texas to the people of America.

No finer gift is within the reach of any government, or any mortal than the preservation for all time of a vast wilderness area so that the citizens of today, and the generations yet unborn, can view a portion of their native land in its untrammeled natural beauty.

The unselfishness of this great gift, which originated deep in the hearts of the people of Texas, is enhanced by the nobility of the vision that accompanied it. Almost a quarter of a century ago Texans from all walks of life—school children, industrialists, ranchers and housewives—joined in the movement to establish on our southern border a great national park symbolic of the firm friendship that exists between the two great neighboring nations.

Across the border the idea of a Big Bend International Peace Park was received with enthusiasm. Plans were developed in Mexico to set aside a large area of the beautiful mountainous country south of the Rio Grande as a part of the National Park system of Mexico.

Men of good will in both countries remain dedicated to carrying that inspiring ideal forward. I hope sincerely that the day will not be far distant when our mutual hopes can be realized. I have been cheered by recent reports of the constructive volunteer work being done by members of the International Good Neighbor Council. I hope soon to hear of renewed efforts by the International Park and Forestry Commission to make the International Peace Park a reality.

On our northern border the international boundary joins

Glacier National Park with Waterton Lakes National Park on the Canadian side. In 1932 under authority of the Congress and the Canadian parliament they were joined as a symbol of international peace and friendship.

The long unfortified boundaries that the United States shares with its neighbors to the north and south are unique in the history of great nations. The pooling and mutual sharing of great scenic treasures along those borders is an inspiring example to the troubled peoples behind the iron and bamboo curtains of the way free men and women can live in peace and friendship.

Travelers to this scenic wonderland often report they are impressed by the serenity and peace of mind they find here. The towering mountains, the great canyons, and the sleepy winding river and the vast expanse of sunny semi-desert land combine in an atmosphere of tranquillity and peace.

True, the land is peaceful now, and always shall be, but it was not always so.

The Big Bend Country has a record of violence dating back hundreds of millions of years. These very mountains are products of the time when the earth twisted in an anguish of upheaval and volcanic explosions. The plains tell the story of the great floods when the land sank below the sea and of the times when dinosaurs lived here.

In the caves can be found traces of an Indian civilization that thrived before Christ was born and then vanished. The old Comanche Trail crossing the park tells of the fierce plains horsemen who rode a thousand miles from the north to raid the peaceful settlements in Old Mexico. Across this land came the Spanish explorers in search of gold.

Later came the pioneers. Cattle rustlers and outlaws came to prey upon them. Flags of six nations—Spain, France, Mexico, Republic of Texas, Confederate States, and the United States have flown over this land.

Now, as one visitor told the Park Service, there is a something about the Big Bend that makes it different from any other park—it is, he said, the feeling of a friendly warmth that runs like a song through the land. Now this land is consecrated to the ways of peace. Peace came to this wild country when free men settled down and learned under democracy to live with one another as neighbors.

Among the early teachers of the virtues of law and order and the principles of good neighborliness was Captain Everett Ewing Townsend, to whom all of us are forever indebted for the part he played in paving the way for the establishment of Big Bend National Park.

As a young Texas Ranger he rode into the Big Bend Country, searching for cattle rustlers before the turn of the century. He never forgot the beauty of the land he saw there.

Many years later while serving in the Texas Legislature he sponsored legislation to establish a state park here. Then he began to work on the idea of having it become a national park. He found strong supporters, including Dr. Horace Morelock and the late Amon Carter.

It is not easy for any area to obtain national park status. That is why only 28 of the 181 areas in the National Park System can bear that proud title.

Each national park must possess qualities distinctive enough to make its preservation a matter of concern to the whole nation.

The Park Service experts found that Big Bend had more than its share of these qualities.

And so, on June 20, 1935, Congress authorized the establishment of Big Bend National Park when the necessary land had been obtained.

Texans did not ask Uncle Sam to acquire the land. Private citizens had contributed generously and finally the State Legislature appropriated $1,500,000 and authorized the Texas State Parks Board to acquire by purchase, condemnation or donation all of the remaining acres in the proposed national park area.

In 1944 when title to the park land was turned over to the Federal Government it was not easy or comfortable to visit this beautiful wilderness area. The approach roads were rough and subject to washouts. Few comforts aside from the magnificent scenery were available to visitors.

In 1944 only 850 visitors were counted in the park all year. Last year the number of visitors had grown to 81,000. This year that figure has already been surpassed.

Ten years from now—in 1966—the number of visitors to Big Bend will approximate 500,000 according to our National Park Service experts. And this figure will continue to mount.

Look about you in this beautiful Basin and consider for a moment what would happen if half a million people were concentrated here in the course of a single year. Visualize, if you can, the facilities they would require—the roads, lodging, restaurants, gas stations, and other facilities. Clearly, the very beauty that attracted the multitudes soon would be destroyed. To permit this to happen would be a desecration.

It shall not happen. That I can promise.

Yet a way must be found to permit those anticipated half-million citizens to enjoy the beauties of Big Bend. It can be done without despoiling the wild beauty of these mountains.

It will require bold planning and vigorous actions.

The federal government cannot do the job alone. The National Park Service will need public spirited partners. It will need the understanding cooperation of the people of Texas, and particularly those in the neighboring communities. It will need the assistance of private capital to provide the concession facilities necessary for the comfort and convenience of those visitors.

Looking ahead we can visualize the kind of development Big Bend will require to care for its ever-growing number of visitors.

The rugged beauty of the Chisos Mountains will be preserved by restraining over-development. Of course, the facilities now here must be improved and modernized. Park planners feel, however, the construction of roads and the developed area in the Basin has progressed just about as far as it can without harming the scenery.

Future plans contemplate the establishment of an attractive village in an oasis near the river in the vicinity of Hot Springs. Here the Park's principal visitor accommodations would be concentrated. Motels, cabins, stores and other visitor facilities would be created and operated by park concessioners. The Park Service would also install roads, water and sewage facilities and public campgrounds. A spur road would take visitors to the spectacular Mariscal Canyon area. Another development is contemplated for the Santa Elena Canyon area with provisions for expansion to meet the growing needs of the future.

These plans for the future are part of the 10-year program which we are developing to provide the American people with the kind of National Park System they want.

We call this program "MISSION 66" because we hope to reach its objectives in 1966 when the National Park Service will celebrate the golden anniversary of its establishment by Congress.

In my long career as a public official, no duty has been more rewarding or brought me more personal satisfaction than that of exercising stewardship over the parks in which our people find enjoyment. I take justifiable pride in the beautiful parks of my native state of Oregon. As mayor of our capital city of Salem and later as governor of the state, I contributed in some measure to their development and expansion.

"MISSION 66," therefore, is a program in which I am intensely interested. I look upon it as one of the most important developments in the entire history of the National Park Service. We are determined to do the very best we can to meet the urgent current needs of the almost overwhelming number of people visiting the parks.

In 1920 the number of visitors to National Park areas totaled one million; in 1940 there were seventeen million. This year the figure will be around fifty million.

When I first came to Washington I found to my dismay that the Park Service was attempting to take care of almost fifty million visitors in a park system developed to handle about half the number. There had been no substantial capital investments in park facilities for more than a decade. The demands of World War II, the Korean War and the cold war had forced curtailments all along the line. The Service was understaffed and its facilities were outmoded and wearing out.

We have made real progress in the last three years. We have increased the appropriations for the National Park Service some 40 per cent from $33 million to $45 million. We have encouraged concessioners to make substantial investments toward improving and expanding the facilities they operate. We have added new land to the system each year. But as visitor demands increased, it became clear that we had to do more than merely try to catch up with the demand. Aggressive action was called for to put the park system in shape to meet future demands which are clearly foreseeable.

In attacking this challenging problem the Park Service retained one basic concept as a guiding beacon in preparing its new program. This was the concept of conservation and use set for it by the Congress when the National Park Service was established.

It decrees that the park areas must be preserved for the benefit and enjoyment of the American people. I want to see the parks kept as open for all of our people as they were when I was a boy. The thought of rationing use of our parks is repugnant to me, as I know it is to you. Yet we must face the hard truth that visitor enjoyment is impaired by masses of people who crowd to the same spot to see the same view at the same time. Natural features are destroyed and historic ruins worn away by the trampling of too many feet.

Rationing the beauty of our parks might be the only solution if we stood still. We can reject such a suggestion only because we are moving forward.

The Big Bend National Park was named for the big bend in the Rio Grande, but it came into being because a lot of big-hearted people in a big state got behind the project in a big way. The job was finally accomplished and a dream became reality with the ceremony on Dedication Day.

It wasn't easy to get title to the vast expanse which lies within the boundaries of the park. In clearing the title to the little parcels of land, some strange history came to light.

Sam Woolford, writing about the region he knows so well, related one of Bob Cartledge's famous stories on land deals in the Big Bend:

"It was up there, coming off of Burro Mesa toward the Rattlesnakes. We found some of that country was cut up into 5- and 10-acre plots. One section was owned by nobody but retired school teachers; the next one would be cut up into tiny building sites owned exclusively by doctors.

"One time three women came to Alpine to look up some of their real estate investments in the Big Bend. Old Judge Van Sickle sent me word that they wanted to inspect their land, and asked me to arrange it. I sent him back a letter and told him that as near as I could figure things out, the land was somewhere up on Burro Mesa, but that neither God nor man could ever locate it—or want it if they did.

"Well, the women came here anyway and looked me up. I showed them on the map about where their plots were located, the general vicinity, that is, but I told them I didn't know how to get to it—even if I knew for sure where it was. They wanted to know what they might do with what they'd bought, and I advised 'em to get a promoter to divide it up again. They could find someone just as eager as they'd been to own a little chunk of earth; lots of people are land-hungry enough to buy first and hunt for it later."[3] A whole volume could be written on clearing the deed to the Big Bend National Park.

---

3. Sam Woolford, "Tales of the Big Bend," San Antonio *Light,* March 27, 1955, p. 19A.

Chapter 3

PLACE NAMES IN THE PARK

THE *PLACE NAMES* in the park itself are the ones which will be wondered about, asked about and become known to increasing numbers of people. As the park is developed, more and more places will be named. To interpret the region more clearly to visitors, we have told not only the story of how the places acquired their names but the details of incidents which happened at those places. Of such incidents is woven the fabric of the region's history and they give it a texture all its own.

The hub of the park region is made up of a group of mountains called the Chisos. Like spokes radiating from a hub, the trails and roads lead from the Chisos to the many points of interest or to the main highways crossing the country. Along the roads and trails there are mountains, springs, canyons and other landmarks, with names based on fact and legend. But the Chisos will be the beginning point for most tourists, and the name is an old one with few published facts and much romantic legend to explain its origin.

One legend has it that "Chisos" means ghosts and certainly the high serrated cliffs have a ghostly appearance when viewed from a distance. Substantiating the ghost legend is the story of the ghost of Alsate, an Indian chief. As the legend goes, back in 1880 a tribe of Mescalero Apaches, driven southward by their enemies, the Comanches, made their last stand in the Chisos Mountains. Facing them across the Rio Grande was another enemy, the Mexicans, whose ranches and villages they raided at every opportunity. Finally a man came to Chief Alsate with a message from the commanders at San Carlos, inviting the entire tribe to a great *fiesta*. Wary, but intrigued by the glowing promises of gifts and food, the Apaches went into the Mexican town, got gloriously drunk and waked up the next morning in chains. Right away they were marched to the interior and distributed as slaves among the Mexicans. But Alsate and his squaw managed to escape and it was believed that they returned to the stronghold in the Chisos. Soon stories of ghosts in the Chisos were circulated and the Mexicans, who had rejoiced because their enemies, the Apaches, had been exterminated, became afraid, and the *rattero* or stool pigeon who had invited Alsate and his tribe to San Carlos was so scared that he left the country.

These ghosts were unusual because they left footprints, and for that reason they came to be called "Big Foot and Little Foot." There are those who said they had seen the two Indians. The apparitions were unarmed and fearful of anyone who tried to approach them. But when food was placed outside their cave, it was always gone in the morning. Some say that an American killed the Indians at Stillwell Crossing and others declared that the skeleton of Alsate was found in the Chisos in a cave which became known as the Cuevo de Alsate.

But historians give perhaps the most accurate origin of the name of the Chisos Mountains and their account pre-dates the legend of Alsate by almost two hundred years.

It was in the year 1688 that the Governor of Nueva Viscaya ordered General Juan de Retana to set out with ninety Spaniards and a number of friendly Indians to make war upon the Chisos Indians until they agreed to congregate in settlements assigned to them. They were regarded as the kingdom's worst enemies. These Indians were then living in *rancherias* in the vicinity of the Chisos Mountains.

Don Santiago was a chief among the Chisos Indians and some of the old Mexicans say that Santiago Peak was named for him, but another legend about the naming of that famous peak has been told for generations and cannot be disregarded (see page 68). The Spaniards fought an all-day battle with Don Santiago, who finally offered to surrender after he had lost a number of his followers, both men and women. In the Indian camp, the Spaniards found loot which had been taken from the Spaniards in Coahuila. They also rescued a Spanish captive who had been taken in the same raid. He was a boy of twelve and he told about a little girl who had been captured with him. He said that as soon as they arrived in the Indian camp, the old women of the tribe killed and ate the little girl. So the Chisos Indians were called cannibals.

Another account of the origin of the name "Chisos" comes from romantic Mexico. In Mexico City, on August 26, 1955, Lic. Antonio Fernandez del Castillo, Secretary and Treasurer of the National Academy of History and Geography, spoke to a meeting of government officials, their guests and friends about a subject of interest to those on both sides of the Rio Grande. His subject was entitled: "Marvelous Landscape of the Rio Grande in the Big Bend." He described the poor roads and the uninteresting scenery on his trip from Marathon toward the Big Bend Park. He said, "True, that after traveling more than fifty kilometers we had not encountered anything else worth looking at, even though we were already in the Big Bend Park. But continuing our bumpy ride a little longer, we began to see at the right a great bulk which proclaimed the site called the Casa Grande, which forms part of the Chizo Mountains. Casa Grande, which dominates the major part of the Sierra, is so called because of its peculiar shape which gives the impression of an old abandoned castle still showing its turrets on the main wall. The name of the mountain range bears its Castillian origin in the word 'hechizos,' meaning enchantment.

"Nothing is more proper than that name for a mountain in a solitary place where there are heard no noises but the trill of the birds and the murmer of the wind evoking fantastic legends about that fortress created by the centuries as a result of erosion. As far as one can see, the rising sun tints the view an intense, vivid red. On the other hand, at night the mountain stands out like a silver castle in a Medieval night of enchantment."

Whether or not the mountains were named for the Chisos Indians who lived there, or the Indians were called Chisos or Chizos because they lived in the mountains by that name, is still a point in question, but the quotation above is a likely explanation as to "how come it's called that."

Dr. Elton Miles, Professor of English, Sul Ross State College presented a paper entitled "Chisos Ghosts" to the Texas Folklore Society in Dallas, April 13, 1957, in which he said, "I am of the opinion that the meaning of 'Chisos' ultimately is 'People of the Forest' and that these people, the Chisos Indians, were Apaches. Intensive study of records and extensive correspondence with Indian linguists and ethnologists, reveals that a widespread Indian word for the Apache is *chishi* (pronounced chish-ee). It is to be found in the languages of the Lagunero, Lipan, Navaho, and Tewa, all of which are Apachean. The Lagunero and the Lipan were adjoining neighbors of the Chiso in the Big Bend. It appears that Chizos, later spelled Chisos, is a Spanish pluralization of the Apachean word *chishi* which means 'people of the forest.' "

Still another likely explanation for the name "Chisos" comes from Dr. Frederick J. Dockstader, Assistant Director of the Museum of the American Indian, New York City, who says:

> *"I have gone over what little material there is on these people, but have had no luck as yet in running down the definite meaning of the name. I do know this:*
>
> *"The Chizos are not Apache, although this is often locally applied to them. They are related to the Concho people, and are a sub-division of the large Uto-Aztekan linguistic family (whereas the Apache are all related within the Athapascan linguistic group).*
>
> *"As I recall your story of the local name, there was a claim that* chizos *means* ghosts, *right? This I am inclined to doubt. It is true that in some of the*

Apachean dialects, chindi *(or related forms) means evil spirits, ghosts, devils . . . . but it would then have to follow that the name was applied to them by the Apache, which could certainly be in the realm of possibility. The term* chindi'tzoh *means* evil water *in Apache, but where this would apply, I do not know; it is the only "zoh" ending I can think of.*

"More likely, it seems to me, is that the term may have a relationship to the Spanish. Since the Chizos were mountainous people, it would not be peculiar if they were called chivos *by the Spanish . . . . this slang term, meaning* goats, *not only makes sense, but could readily become transformed into Chizos . . . just as* goats *can be transformed into* ghosts.

"Quién sabe?"[1]

In the center of the principal Chisos group is a basin like a stupendous stadium from which to view the surrounding peaks and mountains. The Basin was called that because no other name so aptly describes its form. Within the Basin are today located the tourist accommodations and one important source of the water supply. The Big Bend is a desert country and good drinking water is an important commodity. In fact there likely would be no Big Bend National Park today if water had not been discovered in the well in the Basin. That well is called Agua Pronto (Spanish words for "Water! Quick!") and "how come it's called that" is the story of the beginning of the park project.

Several wells had been dug in Green Gulch, but they didn't draw enough water to interest a dirt dauber. The Chamber of Commerce at Alpine had spent about all they had, along with the donations made by all the Big Bend civic clubs, in trying to get the CC Camp established. All those working with the project thought water could be found in

1. Taken from a letter from Dr. Frederick J. Dockstader to Virginia Madison, July 25, 1957.

the Basin, so they made their location there, set up the equipment and started digging. After a few hours they drew out the first bucket of water and by night the water was flowing so fast they couldn't dig and bail at the same time. Back in camp were a pump and pipe which were moved to the new well site early the next morning. Pretty soon the pump was going and the water level lowered enough to allow digging to be resumed. They got water quick (Agua Pronto), called the well that, and the next month the CC Camp was located there. The CCC boys did some developmental work, visiting delegations came in and before long the whole country began hearing reports of what could be seen in the fabulous Big Bend Country. This remote frontier land was being invaded as it never had been invaded before.

From the Basin, a number of the Chisos Mountains and peaks are visible. Casa Grande, so named because it resembles a big house or an old castle, is one of the best known and most often photographed of the Chisos Mountains, and to one couple Casa Grande became known as the House of Romance. Once a delegation of Highway 67 boosters on a trip to Chihuahua City stopped in the Big Bend National Park to spend the night. In the group was a Cleburne, Texas, couple—a newspaper editor and a business woman, whose long acquaintance had produced nothing more than a neutral relationship. They spoke, but no sparks sputtered. During the evening, along with several others, they climbed the trail high up the side of Casa Grande. The stars "hung low and eminent." The moonlight cast its spell and the couple realized they were in love. After the tour they were married and from all reports are living happily together. For them, old Casa Grande will always be *Casa de Amor,* or the House of Romance.

The highest peak of the Chisos group as seen from the Basin is Mt. Emory, named for Major William H. Emory,[2]

2. William H. Emory, *Report of the U. S.–and Mexican Boundary Survey,* A. O. P. Nicholson, Printer, Washington, 1857. Vol. I, Chapter v, p. 83.

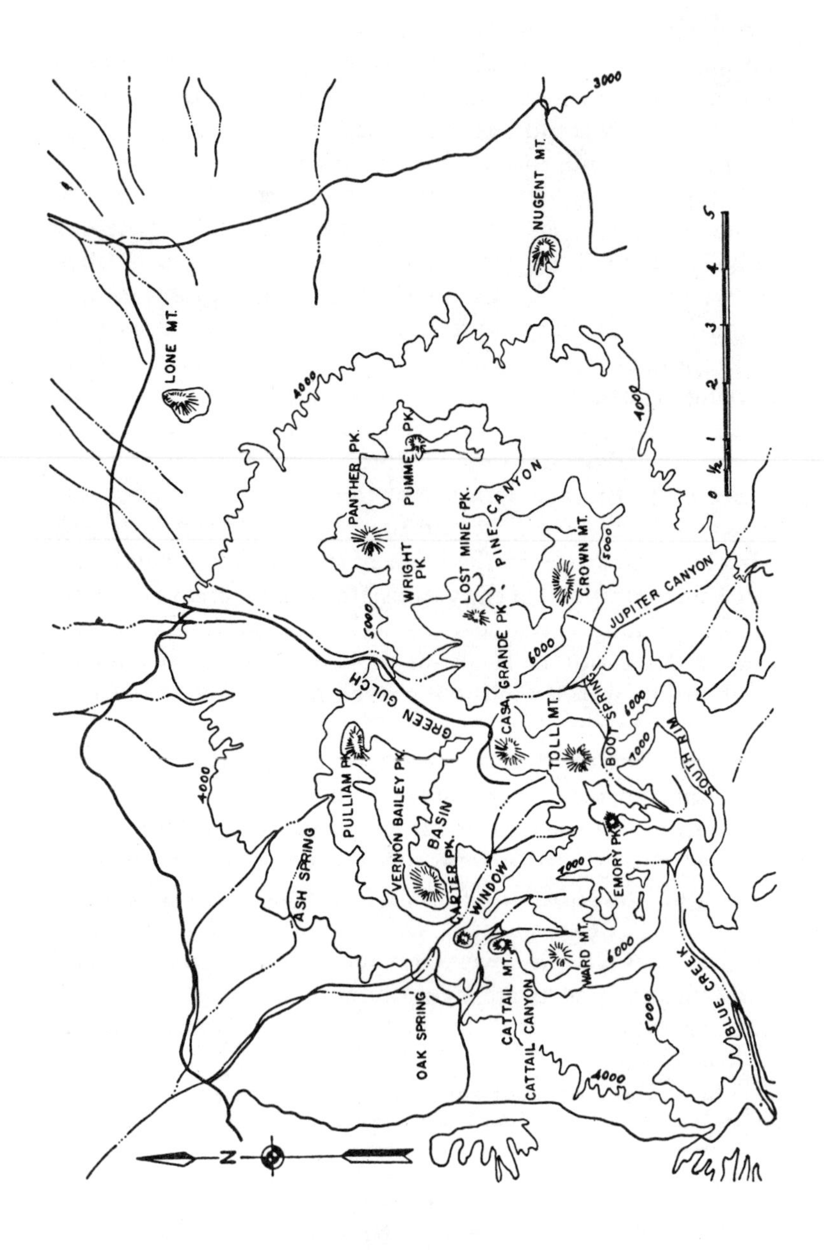
LONE MT.
NUGENT MT.
3000
4000
PANTHER PK.
PUMMEL PK.
WRIGHT PK.
LOST MINE PK.
PINE CANYON
CROWN MT.
5000
JUPITER CANYON
CASA GRANDE PK.
6000
GREEN GULCH
TOLL MT.
BOOT SPRING
7000
SOUTH RIM
PULLIAM PK.
VERNON BAILEY PK.
BASIN
CARTER PK.
WINDOW
EMORY PK.
ASH SPRING
WARD MT.
CATTAIL MT.
CATTAIL CANYON
OAK SPRING
BLUE CREEK
N
0 ½ 1 2 3 4 5

head of the United States–Mexican Boundary Commission which established the Rio Grande as the boundary line between the United States and Mexico. The name was proposed by the surveyors who worked in the Big Bend in 1852 on the boundary survey. They thought it was fitting to honor their leader in this way.

From the Basin the best view of the surrounding country is seen through the Window, a great gap between Ward Mountain and Vernon Bailey Peak. Ward Mountain was named for Johnnie Ward who camped at Ward Spring at the base of the mountain when he was working for the G-4 outfit. Vernon Bailey Peak was named to honor the eminent naturalist who died in April, 1942. He had done biological work in Texas over a period of fifty years and had made several expeditions to the Big Bend region. The peak was called Old Baldy for a time but was changed by the Park Service about 1944.

The newest place name in Big Bend National Park is Carter Peak, approved by the U. S. Board on Geographic Names on August 29, 1957. This peak is the spectacular target in the gunsight of the Window, and is separated from Ward Mountain by Cattail Falls, an entrancing beauty spot in a wild and almost inaccessible canyon.

Carter Peak is often the focal point for cameras aimed at the vast panorama of mountains, mesas, desert and yet more mountains, falling away from the Window.

More people in the world know of the man for whom the peak is named than at this time know of Big Bend National Park, but in time people everywhere will visit the park, thus bringing to fruition the dream and hope of the late Amon G. Carter, Sr., who believed that the Big Bend country has much to offer visitors to Texas and worked as long as he lived to provide and protect for them a playground of spectacular beauty and magnitude. The choice of this peak to bear the name of one of Texas' most noted citizens is a wise one, for no visitor leaves the park without looking through the Window which frames Carter Peak and opens out to the scene which stretches past the Rio Grande into the land of Mexico. And when one stands alone with his thoughts, it is fitting that he should know something of the story behind "How Come It's Called That."

The name, Carter Peak, was proposed by members of the National Park Service, and the reason for the proposition was expressed by a former superintendent of the Big Bend park when he said, "We all know of Mr. Carter's sincere interest in the Big Bend National Park and his leadership in having it created. In fact, without Mr. Carter, I believe there would not have been any Big Bend National Park." Though this official had never met Mr. Carter, he had learned from the Park Service files something of the moves which had actually put the project across and he had found Amon G. Carter actively identified with every movement to bring about the purchase, establishment and dedication of Big Bend National Park. He put his strength, his money and his organizational know-how behind the job, and when the work was done he went to Washington, as personal representative of the Governor of Texas, to hand the deed to the park lands to President Roosevelt. This he did on historic D-Day, June 6, 1944.

But there remained much to be done to make Big Bend National Park a going concern, and Amon G. Carter continued to work toward that end. Through his paper, the Fort Worth *Star-Telegram,* he gave publicity to every person, place and project that had to do with the advancement of the Park's interest. His death came at 8:20 P.M., June 23, 1955, just a few months before Dedication Day. Guests at the Dedication ceremony in the Basin on November 21, 1955, heard tribute paid to the late Amon G. Carter, Sr. and no doubt every one of them at some time during the day looked out to the scene beyond the Window and caught a glimpse of the peak, then unnamed, which shall serve as a lasting tribute to that great individualist.

It is impossible to write briefly of a man who has done so much for so many, but a thumbnail characterization of the man who was admittedly self-made and who rose to a position of wealth and power can be found in the remarks of one of his employees who said, "Amon Carter not only started from scratch but he scratched out a place to make a start from.— Money to him was more of something to lift others up with than to hoard for himself."

Books can and will be written about Amon G. Carter and his achievements, but for the purpose of knowing how come Carter Peak is called that, we note these events upon which to hang our memories of the man.

Amon Giles Carter, Fort Worth publisher and philanthropist, was born December 11, 1879, in a log house at Crafton in Wise County, Texas. He was forced to make his own way in the world when he was eleven years old, after the death of his mother, and was almost entirely self-educated, although he was able to attend public school for a time while employed as a handy boy in a small-town hotel. He learned the rudiments of salesmanship, which became his forte, by selling sandwiches to train passengers at Bowie, Texas. When, at eighteen, he took to the road selling photographic enlargements, he was so successful that the owners gave him the company to avoid the staggering outlay his commissions called for. Later he got a job with a San Francisco advertising firm. He returned to Texas in 1905 to start an advertising agency of his own, but soon found himself in the newspaper business. In 1906 he and Col. Louis J. Wortham, early-day editor and Texas historian, bought the Fort Worth *Star*. In 1909 they acquired the Fort Worth *Telegram* and merged the two newspapers. He became publisher of the *Star-Telegram* in 1923 and made it and himself widely known throughout the United States and abroad. He was proudest of the achievements his prestige made possible for his city and his state, and especially for West Texas, which he and his newspaper primarily served. The *Star-Telegram* proclaims Fort Worth to be "Where the West Begins." For better living and cultural conditions in Fort Worth and West Texas he lavishly gave of time, money and effort, and many institutions acknowledged him as principal benefactor. He helped to establish Texas Technological College at Lubbock and was its first board Chairman. He was a prime mover in the building of the coliseum where Fort Worth's famous Southwestern Exposition and Fat Stock Show is held, and named it for his intimate friend, Will Rogers. He was one of the organizers of the Trinity River Authority; was chiefly responsible for Fort Worth's airport, conceded to be one of the world's finest; he helped to organize one of the nation's major airlines and was an important West Texas oil producer. And for his part in bringing into being Big Bend National Park, he was one of the eight men awarded honorary commissions as national park ranger at a ceremony in the Chisos Mountains Basin, July 28, 1954.[3]

The spectacular erosive spires of Pulliam Peak are among the most beautiful in the Chisos group. Pulliam Peak was named for a pioneer rancher, Bill Pulliam, who is reported to have ranched at more places in the Big Bend than any other man, but his name is attached to this one place only. Old-timers refer to Pulliam Bluff as the scene of this story. It was said of Bill Pulliam that he would give his family anything within his power to give them. When his wife wanted a log cabin, Bill set about getting the pine logs to build it.

---

3. "Awards of honorary park ranger commissions on wood-burned leather scrolls have been announced by the National Park Service to Amon G. Carter of Fort Worth, president of the Big Bend National Park Association; Dr. Horace W. Morelock, former president of Sul Ross College, and former State Senator Benjamin Franklin Berkeley, both of Alpine and both vice presidents of the association; U. S. District Judge R. E. Thomason of El Paso, former member of the National House and author of the bill creating the Big Bend National Park; former State Senator H. L. Winfield of Fort Stockton, who steered legislation through the Legislature appropriating funds for park land purchases; Frank D. Quinn, present chairman of the State Park Board and former executive secretary of the board; James E. Casner of Alpine, who worked as a private citizen at his own expense for creation of the park, and the late Capt. E. E.

Above his camp was the bluff which now bears his name, and it was then covered with a heavy growth of large pines. He built a cable to the top of the bluff and lowered the logs to the cabin site at its base. At first the cable was faulty in operation and the logs landed too hard and splintered, but Bill Pulliam finally perfected his cable and the logs arrived at the cabin site intact. A portion of the walls of the cabin he built still stands as evidence of Bill Pulliam's ingenuity.

Falling away from and immediately below the Window is Oak Canyon, named for the magnificent growth of oaks there. Through the Window one can get an excellent view of Terlingua, approximately nineteen miles away as the crow flies, and on clear days (and most of them *are* clear) one can see for one hundred miles across the Rio Grande into Mexico. The area viewed through the Window is the Big Bend's potential treasure chest, for it is rich in minerals.

The only way to get a better view of the surrounding outside world than that seen from the Window is to climb to the South Rim of the Chisos. This trip has to be made on horseback—about seven miles from the Basin to an elevation of over 7,000 feet. On the way to the South Rim you pass Mt. Emory (7,835 feet) on the left of the trail, and go on to Boot Spring which is in Boot Canyon, just above Boot Rock which is shaped like a huge stone boot and sticks out like a sore thumb to goad sightseers into asking "How come it's called that?" Juniper Canyon and Spring are two or three miles southeast of Boot Canyon and both are named for the many juniper trees which grow in that vicinity.

When the traveler reaches the South Rim *via* the South Rim Trail, he will have to adjust his vision to distance for

---

Townsend, former Texas Ranger and legislator, who was one of the first to urge creation of a national park encompassing the Chisos Mountains. He was the first commissioner of the Big Bend National Park.

"The award to Carter will be made in absentia and that to Captain Townsend will be presented to his widow." Fort Worth *Star-Telegram,* July 25, 1954.

he can see far into Mexico. Because this rim rock is on the south side of the highest side of the Chisos, it is called South Rim. From this great natural stage one can see interesting peaks and canyons and little settlements.

The first time one looks out from the South Rim, he will see the vastness, the coloring, and the ruggedness. He will also feel small and unimportant. The effect of the Big Bend panorama on a stranger to the region is perfectly described by the noted author and artist, Ludwig Bemelmans. "Leaving Highway 90 at Marathon, we came to the Big Bend country toward sunset, that part of Texas where the Rio Grande makes a U-shaped bend in its course. In a lifetime spent in traveling, here I came upon the greatest wonder. The mantle of God touches you; it is panorama without beginning or end.

"No fire can burn so bright, no projection can duplicate the colors that dance over the desert or the bare rock formations that form the backdrop. No words can tell you, and no painter hold it. It is only to be visited and looked at with awe. It will make you breathe deeply whenever you think of it, for you have inhaled eternity."[4]

Captain E. E. Townsend, Texas Ranger, said the same thing in fewer words back in 1894 when he noted in his scout book, "It made me see God as I had never seen Him before."

From this vantage point on the South Rim, one can see almost the entire spread of the proposed park in Mexico, which when completed, will become an International Park. So clear is the atmosphere that the faraway mountains in Mexico seem to be within walking distance. There they are: the Sierra del Carmen; Pico Centinela (meaning Sentinel Peak), which is the highest point in Coahuila; Fronteriza; Sierra de San Vicente; and Sierra Ponca; all different in coloring and contour.

On the Texas side of the river you can see Tortuga Mountain. *Tortuga* is Spanish for the word turtle, and the moun-

---

4. Ludwig Bemelmans, "The Texas Legend," *McCall's* Magazine, August, 1956, p. 24.

tain does resemble the head of a turtle. Chilicotal Mountain is covered with a shrub called *chilicote,* which bears a little berry or bean which the Mexicans sometimes use as a substitute for chili pepper or chili powder. A thicket of the *chilicote* shrubs is called *chilicotal,* and from them the mountain gets its name.

The beautiful gorge carved into the eastern wall of the Chisos is known to the old-timers as Wade Canyon and was named for Lloyd Wade who introduced the first bathtub into the Chisos. Because the canyon is filled with beautiful pine trees, it is also called Pine Canyon. But those who remember how much trouble Lloyd Wade had in getting his bathtub to his home in the canyon, prefer to call it Wade Canyon.

Estufa Canyon in this vicinity was so named because John Rice left an old stove there when he moved to Chilicotal. *Estufa* is the Spanish word for stove and those seeing the abandoned stove there began to call the place Estufa Canyon. The name remained long after the stove was gone.

On the south end of Chilicotal Mountain is Glenn Springs, called that because an old settler by that name lived there. He grazed a herd of horses in that section and to provide a better water supply for his horses, he dug out the springs. It is reported that Indians or Mexicans killed him near the spring which still bears his name. Researchers have discovered that long before Mr. Glenn's herd of horses grazed in the vicinity of Glenn Springs, a herd of Dinosauria grazed there.

Glenn Springs has had a turbulent history. Not only was the man for whom the springs were named murdered there, but in 1916, while officials of both countries were engaged in a peace conference in El Paso, a couple of Mexican bandits with a large following of *compadres* raised plenty of cain at Glenn Springs before high-tailing it across the Rio Grande into Mexico.

These bandits moved from Torreon to the Rio Grande, recruiting additional men all the way. Political affiliation made no difference for Carranzistas and Villistas both joined.

On Cinco de Mayo (May 5th), an important Mexican holiday, these bandits crossed the Rio Grande where they were joined by relatives and friends on the Texas side. No one thought anything about their appearance in gradually increasing numbers because the occasion was an important one and celebrators were expected. By eleven o'clock that night several hundred bandits moved against the little settlement of Glenn Springs, then garrisoned by eight or nine soldiers of the Fourteenth Infantry in charge of Sergeant Smythe. The attackers tied their horses some distance from the settlement and crept forward on foot.

Two soldiers were on guard and the others asleep, three inside the adobe quarters and the rest outside because the night was hot. The bandits attacked, yelling "*Viva Carranza y Viva Villa.*" For several hours the handful of soldiers withstood the attackers but the bandits had planned their campaign well. They knew that the soldiers' quarters were covered with a thatching of *candelilla* and that it burned like powder so they threw balls of twine and red flannel soaked in kerosene and in full blaze onto the *candelilla* thatched roofs. The soldiers were burned out, and in trying to escape three were killed, one was seriously wounded and the others were severely burned.

Living at the settlement then were W. K. Ellis and his wife; C. G. Compton, who clerked in the Ellis Store; and Mr. Compton's three children, a four-year-old boy, a girl, and a boy of ten who was a deaf-mute. A few Mexican families lived in scattered *jacals*. At the beginning of the raid, the younger Compton boy was killed, and Mr. Compton escaped, carrying his little daughter. He left the deaf-mute child behind because he knew that the Mexicans were afraid to harm a handicapped person—it was one of their superstitions. The child was not harmed.

The bandits looted the store and the home. When the Ellis couple heard the shooting, they hid out in the canyon back of their house and walked for twelve miles to the John Rice ranch. The bandits ransacked the Ellis home, taking all of

Mrs. Ellis' beautiful clothes, but left her silverware in the bottom of her trunk. Mrs. Ellis had come to Glenn Springs as a bride, and her wedding presents and trousseau delighted the looters, who had never seen such finery. The next day some of the bandits were seen near San Vicente wearing Mrs. Ellis' hats and carrying her elegant parasols on horseback. They were having a hell of a good time.

During the battle that night, neighbors at a ranch about three miles away heard the shooting and went to investigate. Captain C. D. Wood at first thought it was a Cinco de Mayo celebration, but when the shooting continued he awakened Oscar de Montel, who was staying at Wood's house, and together they started to Glenn Springs. The night was pitch-dark and they got off the road and into a cactus flat. It took them almost three hours to reach Glenn Springs. They were within fifty yards of the store when they heard horses eating corn and Mexicans talking.

De Montel started up a hill to get a better view of the flaming buildings when some one said, *"¿Quién vive?"* When De Montel asked *"¿Quién es?"* the shooting started. Wood and De Montel took off like scared jackrabbits and ran into a wire fence which knocked them flat on their backs. A bullet hit a rock at Captain Wood's feet and shattered fragments of rock struck his hand. He thought he was shot, but didn't stop to see how seriously. When the two were out of the range of gunfire they stopped and hid until morning. The raiders left before daylight and Wood and De Montel went down to help the soldiers, who were terribly burned. Captain Wood said that they had blisters as large as a man's hand all over their bodies.

The bandits who raided Glenn Springs gathered up their loot and their dead and rode to Boquillas, Texas, where they joined those who had raided the Jesse Deemer store and the ones who had captured the miners and the mine payroll at the Del Carmen mines at Boquillas, Mexico.

The peace conference in El Paso was halted when news of the Glenn Springs raid was received on Sunday. Colonel

Langhorne and the Eighth Cavalry were ordered to follow the bandits into Mexico and to return the American captives and American property. But by the time the news had reached El Paso and the army could march to Boquillas, the bandits had four days' start on them and were long gone. The captives were abandoned at El Peño because the bandits didn't want to meet with the United States Army while holding captives.

Carranza raised sand about the army being on Mexican soil, and President Wilson ordered Langhorne to return to the Texas side of the Rio Grande. The bandits were never punished but most of the loot was recovered and the captives were returned unharmed. But Mrs. Ellis' hats and parasols remained in Mexico.

After the raid at Boquillas and Glenn Springs, Texan tempers were pretty hot and a lot of good men would have been shot if Roy Stillwell had not been on hand to give a clean bill of health to some of the Mexicans in the vicinity. The Texans were mad because the little Compton boy had been killed and because there had been so much destruction of property and life in the raids. Their impulse was to shoot all Mexicans on sight. The lead editorial written by W. J. Newsom, editor of the local paper, the Marathon *Hustler,* May 13, 1916, had this to say about the tense situation on the border after the bandit raids: "Men joke and laugh in the presence of death and destruction, and there is no such thing as murder. Every man would think he was honored to be detailed to fire the fatal shot that would send some raider to his death. There is an element of Justice running through it all that takes away all sense of barbarism; but there is only two words in every man's mind, 'Kill and Revenge.' And heaven help the Mexican that can't show a clean record."

Because Roy Stillwell had been raised in those parts and knew that most of the Mexicans on the Texas side of the river were as innocent as the Texans, he saved the lives of men who were not involved by reasoning with those who had become trigger-happy.

Immediately after the raids, all the Mexicans in the vicinity were rounded up for questioning, and Jim Walker and Jim Shoemake were told to guard them. Jim Walker reported that he didn't have a gun, so one was rustled up for him. It was a make he knew nothing about and he said that if he had been forced to use it he probably would have shot himself. However, he did what he was told and the two Jims guarded the Mexicans all night. Later he learned that the gun he had used wouldn't even shoot, but the Mexicans didn't know that and they were careful not to provoke the angry Texans.

After the Glenn Springs and Boquillas raids, Mexicans in the lower Big Bend country had to have letters of recommendation or some proof that they were not connected with the raiders if they wanted to work or even stay on the Texas side of the river. Horace Benson wrote such a letter for one of the Mexicans working for him. That letter probably did more than laws and government edicts to bring about better relations between the Mexicans and the Texans. Whenever the Mexican was questioned about his right to be in Texas, he proudly produced his letter which read as follows:

> *To whom it may concern:*
>
> *Juan is cutting sotol for me. When I'm through with him, I'll shoot the ——— —— — ——— myself!*
>
> *Yours truly,*
>
> *Horace Benson*

The Mexican couldn't read or write, had no ill feeling toward anyone, and when a ranchman or ranger stopped him for questioning he produced the letter, which in turn produced a big laugh. He would laugh too, put the letter back into his pocket and go on his way. Few men are killed by their fellow men when the one with the gun is enjoying a good laugh. The Big Bender's marvelous sense of humor paved the way for friendly relations between men of good will on both sides of the Rio Grande and has settled many disputes.

The name Boquillas means "little mouths" and the place was so-named because of the narrowness of the canyon with its straight up-and-down walls of almost two thousand feet. Boquillas is a name applied to a small settlement on the Texas side of the river and to a Mexican village across the river and to the narrow and beautiful canyon in the Rio Grande. In that canyon in a small spring there is a small mosquito fish, the Boquillas mosquito fish, which is found in no other waters in the world.

Boquillas, Mexico, from a distance seems to be right at the base of Shot Tower. There are several versions of the story as to "how come Shot Tower is called that." 1) The peak resembles the tower or instrument used in making lead shot and some think the name came from that source. 2) A German geologist by the name of Schott did some work in that region and some say that it was named for him but that the spelling was changed.[5] 3) Others say it was named Shot Tower because there is a round hole at the top of the peak which is believed to have been made by a ball discharged from a cannon—therefore it is a "shot tower."

Once there was a discussion among the Americans employed at the mines located near the peak as to whether or not it could be climbed. One daring fellow said he could climb it and offered to bet five hundred pesos that he could. The wager was accepted by his co-workers and one Saturday evening he set out. He had agreed to prove his success by lighting a fire on top of the peak. After several hours the fire was seen on top of Shot Tower. Some time early next morning the mountain climber returned to the mining camp and collected his bet. But the fire continued to burn, ultimately razing a large section of the mountains. Shortly thereafter, Mexican

5. Arthur Schott was assistant surveyor with the United States Boundary Commission and it was likely his name which was given to this tower. William H. Emory, *Report of the U. S.–Mexican Boundary Survey, op. cit.,* p. 15.

authorities made the company pay a fine of twenty-five hundred pesos for destroying the grass. This episode had nothing to do with the naming of the peak, but it is an incident to remember when you look at the stony height and calculate whether or not you could climb it.

D. E. Lindsey brought in a wagonload of supplies from San Antonio to stock the trading post which he established at Boquillas, Texas, in 1894. His first customer was a Mexican woman from *el otro lado,* who had to be carried across the Rio Grande by two Mexicans on account of high water. However, water in the Rio Grande was not always too high to cross and the cable bucket that was used on a cable from the silver mines in Mexico was handy for human transportation, so the trading post flourished. Soon a village grew up around the Lindsey store and trade increased to such an extent that Charlie Hess of Marathon bought in as a partner in the business. The partnership of the two young bachelors was a happy and successful one.

Lindsey was a handsome, young border merchant who was naturally included on the guest lists for the social activities in the Big Bend. During a big *baille* some distance into the interior of Mexico, Lindsey was attracted by one of the most beautiful Mexican girls he had ever seen. When love strikes in the Big Bend, it strikes like lightning; so it was that after the first glance at the beautiful girl, Mr. Lindsey knew that either he was looking at the future Mrs. Lindsey or he would be a bachelor for life. To prevent such a state of affairs, he sent a note to her father asking permission to marry the lovely girl. The request was granted and in no time at all the beautiful Mrs. Lindsey was at home in Boquillas, Texas.

The confirmed bachelor, Charlie Hess, Lindsey's partner in the mercantile business, thought a woman around the place was a fine kettle of fish so he gracefully withdrew. The Lindseys stayed on for a time and then moved to San Antonio to bring up their family.

Not long after their departure, there came to Boquillas Chata and Juan Sada who made the village famous for fine

Mexican food and genuine hospitality. The wonderful relationship between Chata and the people of the entire Big Bend Country will be remembered as long as there is a Boquillas.

When the Big Bend National Park was nothing but an idea in the minds of civic leaders, Dr. Benjamin F. Berkeley was a prime mover. He owned several tracts of land along the Rio Grande in the vicinity of Boquillas and all of these he donated to the government, with the exception of one section for which he was paid $2.00 an acre for land that had cost him $1.00 an acre. With that small sum as his only profit, he worked for over twenty years toward the development of the Big Bend National Park, paying his own expenses all that time as he drove thousands of miles, attended untold numbers of meetings, and made countless speeches to boost the Park's development. On one section of the Berkeley land there was a lodge called Ojos de Boquillas. The old sign remains among Senator Berkeley's mementos, but the memory of the good times enjoyed at Berkeley Lodge remains in the minds of many Sul Ross ex-students, for every spring Senator Berkeley offered his lodge to the senior class and hundreds went there on their senior trip before graduation. Before long, thousands of visitors will be able to enjoy a visit to this same spot, for it is one of the three areas to be developed.

George Miller, superintendent of the Big Bend National Park, looks forward with much enthusiasm to the development of Rio Grande Village between Hot Springs and Boquillas. The work on the irrigation ditches, landscaping and roads is already underway. Superintendent Miller says that "Under the MISSION 66 program for the National Park Service the goal is to give the American people a park system adequate in all ways necessary for their enjoyment and inspiration . . . a park system so developed, managed and used that our children and our children's children will enjoy to the fullest the values of their great American heritage which the Park Service administers for all people of the nation.

"Under this MISSION 66 program for Big Bend National Park, it is planned to develop the Chisos Mountains Basin, an area along the Rio Grande between Hot Springs and Boquillas, and an area on the west side of the park. The development of these three areas will include all of the accommodations required for taking care of overnight guests. The actual development of these areas will be carried on by the federal government insofar as landscaping, roads, trails, parking areas, water systems, sewer systems, campgrounds, employee housing, utility buildings and related facilities are required.

"At each of these development areas it is proposed to construct a visitor center building where information and interpretive services will be available to all of the visitors so as to make their understanding of and enjoyment of the park more complete. Each of the visitor centers will concentrate its efforts of disseminating information and interpretive services for that particular section of the park."[6]

Boquillas has always been an important name in the Big Bend country, and with hundreds of thousands of people visiting the area each year, it is a name that will become better known all across the country.

East of Boquillas there appear on the map Ernst Gap, Ernst Tank and Ernst Valley, all named for M. A. Ernst, peace officer, storekeeper and postmaster at La Noria (Spanish for The Well) in early days. Mr. Ernst was the man chosen to serve as secretary of the meeting held at Boquillas in December, 1903, to decide on new place names in the Big Bend Country. A few years later on September 27, 1908, Judge Ernst was shot as he was riding through the gap which now bears his name. He died the next day. The place where he was ambushed is now called Deadman's Curve. It is a new name and somewhat a misnomer, for M. A. Ernst did not die there.

---

6. Personal letter from Superintendent George Miller, Big Bend National Park, Texas, to Virginia Madison, September 28, 1956.

Lou Buttrill was one of the first men to talk to Ernst after he was shot, but even Lou, who was one of his best friends, could not get Ernst to tell who shot him. Judge Ernst did tell Lou that he was returning from Boquillas with papers to prove that certain Mexicans had tampered with the United States mail. He would never name the person or persons who were responsible for his death.

A young Mexican who worked for Ernst said that he saw Judge Ernst at Francisco Solis' store in Boquillas, Texas, and asked permission to have a dance that night at the schoolhouse at La Noria. Permission was given, but the dance was never held, for the musicians hired for the event did not show up and the would-be celebrators started home about five o'clock in the afternoon. When the young man was brought in for questioning in connection with the murder, he reported, "About five miles from Boquillas I heard someone call. It was Judge Ernst lying propped up against a dagger (Spanish dagger plant) on the right-hand side of the trail. He held his right hand to his back, trying to stop the blood. He said he had ridden from the Puerta [or Gap] which was about two miles away but he had to get off his horse when his intestines rolled out through the hole torn in his stomach where the bullet which struck him in the back had emerged. He asked me questions and wrote down the answers. He asked me where I had been and if I still had the pistol which he had given me to use when I carried the mail. Then he told me to ride his horse to La Noria and tell his friends Clemente Mena and Logino Hernandez to come for him in the hack, but he did not want his wife to know anything about it. After we brought him back to La Noria he sent me to Boquillas to tell the Customs Officer about it. I don't think he ever had a doctor. Judge Ernst died on Tuesday.[7] It was generally believed that the one who did the shooting had been hired to do so. The assassin was on the hillside to the west of the road

7. Several men living in the Boquillas–La Noria area were taken to Alpine for questioning, but were released.

and shot Judge Ernst in the back." M. A. Ernst was a peace-loving man who would never carry a gun.

Up Tornillo Flat from La Noria is a place called Dugout, so-named because the first house built there was dug into the hillside to form a dugout shelter. When the Greens moved there, they lived for a time in the dugout until they could build a better house. Old-timers say that Dugout was the cultural center of the Chisos because a schoolhouse was located there.

Aaron Green, who lived at Dugout, was nicknamed Noisy because of his aversion to talk. It was a known fact that Noisy had very little to say to anybody. Once he took a comely schoolteacher to a dance at San Vicente—a whole day's trip on horseback—and after dancing all night they spent another whole day on the return trip. Those who knew Noisy well couldn't help wondering what he would say to a pretty girl on a two-day horseback ride, so they asked the girl, knowing full well that they would get nothing out of Noisy.

"On the way down to the dance," she reported, "he said, 'You see that old owl sittin' in that tree?'

"When we passed that same tree next day, Noisy remarked, 'Ain't he got big eyes?' "

It has been said that the Rio Grande runs both hot and cold, and at Hot Springs, not far from Boquillas, the water runs hot, which is how come the place is called Hot Springs. From 1909 until 1942, Mr. and Mrs. J. O. Langford lived there, except for the years during which they abandoned the Big Bend because of the Mexican Revolution. The Big Bend was a dangerous place during those years. After they left the region, there came to Hot Springs that fabulous character, Maggie Smith, godmother to the Mexican people. It is said that Maggie makes her living off the Mexican people of the lower Big Bend Country and then she turns around and gives all she makes back to them in the way of food, clothes, medicine and small luxuries.

One day a young Mexican couple arrived at Maggie's store at Hot Springs. The wife was in the late stages of labor and to help the baby come into the world they had tied around her body some old cotton stockings filled with rocks. One of these loaded stocking chains was around her swollen body just below the breasts and another around her hips. Maggie removed these rock barriers to birth and made a bed in the back of her pickup so that the young mother-to-be could rest as comfortably as possible on the ride to the doctor at Marathon. With Maggie driving and the husband sitting in the back of the truck with his wife, they raced the stork toward Marathon, but lost the race just they they topped the first hill. Maggie returned to Hot Springs with her charges. The situation was too much for the new father. All he could do was to hang his head over the side of the pickup and vomit. Maggie took care of all three and there were no casualties.

The young couple had nothing for their new baby except one tiny jacket and a little cap. Maggie rummaged among her possessions and came up with some baby clothes, kept no doubt through sentiment. But she gave the precious possessions to the young people who needed them so desperately and the new baby was dressed by the experienced hands of Maggie Smith.

When Hot Springs was abandoned by the National Park Service as a health resort and a spa, Maggie Smith moved up the river to San Vicente, a place named for the Presidio and Mission de San Vicente which were established on the Mexican side of the Rio Grande in 1774. The name was given to honor Saint Vincent, the patron saint of the Mission. At San Vicente, Texas, Maggie Smith continued administering to the Mexican people, swapping yarns with those who stopped to see her. A visit with Maggie can be an exciting experience. Now Maggie is located at Boquillas, Mexico, across the Rio Grande from Boquillas, Texas. There she will go on swapping yarns with her friends and helping those who need her at any time. After Maggie had moved from Hot Springs, a young Mexican who had been shot in an argument with another young man rode twelve miles horseback to get to Maggie for help. He had lost a lot of blood and was close to dying when Maggie put him in her car and drove one hundred fifty miles to the hospital at Fort Stockton. That bit of mercy cost Maggie over five hundred dollars, but in telling about it she says, "I'm not worried. He will pay me back when he can. I've never lost a cent on those I've helped." All across the country, when we have talked with those who have been to the Big Bend Country, they invariably come up with, "Say, do you know Maggie Smith?"

"Mariscal" is a name used to designate three places in the Big Bend. Mariscal Canyon is one of the three major canyons in the park. It is ten miles long and about two thousand feet deep. It lies in the very elbow of the Big Bend in the Rio Grande. Mariscal Canyon cuts through a mountain by the same name, and on the north end of this mountain there used to be an old village called Mariscal. The Spanish word *mariscal* means marshal or blacksmith, and some of the local people say that it also means "big shot," or an important person. They say that Mariscal was named for Albino Villa Alfelias, an Indian fighter, whom the Mexicans considered an important person.

In a group of mountains south of the South Rim are Talley Mountain, named for J. M. Talley who farmed and ranched there about 1904, and Elephant Tusk, so-named because it is shaped like the tusk of an elephant. This peak is also called Indianola but no one seems to know why or when that name was applied. In this area there is Cow Heaven, which is supposed to be a new name and applied because of the good grass and large number of cattle which grazed there in the early days, but according to an account from W. D. Burcham, Cow Heaven is an elevated basin between two sharp ridges in which a blade of grass never yet has grown. Jim P. Wilson claimed that he gave the place its name, explaining that "A cow would have to go to Heaven if stranded on that mountain. She could never live there." W. D. Burcham is an oldtimer and familiar with the region and the late Jim P. Wilson was one of the first ranchers in the Big Bend.

The south end of the Chisos is called Punta de la Sierra,

which means "the end of the mountain." And visible for miles around and slightly west of Punta de la Sierra are the Mule Ear Peaks, so-named because they look exactly like mule ears. Just a short distance west of Mule Ear Peaks is a little settlement called Castolon. The old river Mexicans explain "how come it's called that" by saying that in the early days an old man named Castulo lived by a little spring in the vicinity and that the name Castolon was derived from his name. The peak near the settlement has been called Castolon Peak. Its Spanish form, *Cerro Castellan,* is a corruption of the word meaning great castle or castillion, according to one school of thought.

During the border troubles, the Texas Rangers were stationed at Castolon. One Ranger, whose sense of humor was well known in the Big Bend, always kept the Texas flag flying in front of his house. One night he arrested two armed Mexicans and held them for questioning. He handcuffed one to his flagpole and took the other up to the Cartledge store to get Gene Cartledge to interpret for him. When they went back to question the Mexican who had been left tied to the flagpole, the pole was down and the Mexican gone. It was pitch-dark and when they reached the flagpole and found the captive gone, they didn't know which way to go to pick up the trail. But Cartledge's Doberman pinscher bounded down a trail leaving no doubt as to the direction taken by the captive. The Texas Ranger and Gene followed. After stumbling among the cactus and rocks in the dark for some time without finding the handcuffed Mexican, they went home and waited until daylight. The next morning they saw the trail as plain as day going exactly opposite from the direction the Doberman pinscher had led them the night before. The Ranger looked at the fine dog with something more than disgust before he said, "That's the first damn dog I ever saw that pointed with his tail."

Though Castolon is almost deserted now, it was once a post office and an army sub-station.

Santa Elena Canyon in the Big Bend National Park is one

of the main tourist attractions. The Mexicans say that Louis Ramirez, an Indian fighter, named the canyon. He had a goat ranch just above the Johnson Farm, which is named for Elmo Johnson. Ramirez finally moved to the Mexican side of the Rio Grande and founded a new settlement of Santa Elena Nueva. Santa Elena is believed to be named for Saint Helena, a native of Britain. August 18 is her "Feast Day," the day dedicated to her memory. Santa Elena has also been called Puerta Grande by Lt. Echols on his camel trip down the river in search of a location for an army camp. To him, the canyon looked like a great door in the face of the cliff. There are two spellings of the name of the famous canyon and there will always be arguments as to which one is correct. The early maps used the name of Saint Helena and the little Mexican settlement on the banks of the river near the mouth of the canyon was spelled Santa Helena Nueva. Now the maps are using the name Santa Elena. One explanation is that "H" in the Spanish alphabet is silent at the beginning of a word, and people pronounce the name incorrectly if the "H" is used.

Not many tourists will make the trip through the canyon because it is dangerous and filled with almost impassable barriers. They are more likely to rely on the picturesque yarns of bold explorers for a second-hand view from that vantage point.

A number of years ago a party of six made a trip from Polvo (*polvo* is the Spanish word for dust) down the Rio Grande through Santa Elena Canyon. The expedition was made up of a sheriff, a professor, two cowboys, an undertaker, and a preacher—surely preparation for every eventuality. They embarked in two well-equipped boats, but among the crew of varied interests there were no navigators, and at the end of the journey they reported that their equipment was strung out along the bottom of the Rio Grande all the way from Polvo to the last rapid in the Santa Elena Canyon. An interested cattleman in Marfa asked one of the cowboys which profession represented best fitted a person to make the journey.

"The preacher and the undertaker," answered the cowboy without hesitation.

"How do you figure that?" asked the rancher.

"You need the preacher to pray that you get through and the undertaker to handle the situation in case the prayers are not answered."

The mesa which forms the Texas side of the Santa Elena Canyon is called Mesa de Anguila. The Mexicans along the river say that it is called that because Angulo, whom they believe to have been the last Comanche in the region, lived in caves on this mesa and in Santa Elena Canyon. The caves were called Cuevas de Angulo and the mesa derived its name from this source.

Then there are those who claim that this mesa was named for the eagles which nested there and that its name came from the word *aguila,* which is Spanish for eagle. Others say that Mesa de Anguila is Spanish for Mesa of the Eels. Still others believe that the name comes from the Spanish Mesa de Angel (Mesa of the Angels).

Terlingua Creek flows into the Rio Grande at the mouth of Santa Elena Canyon. Legend has it that Terlingua gets its name from two sources. First it is said to be a corruption of the words *tres lenguas* or three languages, Indian, Spanish and English. Second, it is said to refer to the three tongues or three forks of the river. Up Terlingua Creek, about fourteen miles from the Rio Grande, is the ghost town of Terlingua (not in the park), once the capital of the quicksilver district. Now that the quicksilver mines are re-opened and prospectors are swarming all over the region looking for uranium and other minerals, perhaps Terlingua will thrive again.

East of Terlingua looking toward the Chisos hub is Rattlesnake Mountain, so-called because there are many rattlesnakes there and because it seems to be a favorite place for rattlers to hibernate.

Rattlesnake Mountain calls to mind the story of one rattlesnake in that vicinity which had to die twice—first by the bullet from the pistol of an angry cowboy and second, by the sotol stalk club in the hands of a famous photographer.

Texans are mighty proud of their state's historic shrines and scenic grandeur, so when a national magazine sent a photographer to do a series of pictures on Texas, the governor, Coke Stevenson, commissioned Frank Quinn, then chairman of the Texas State Parks Board, to show this photographer the interesting places in Texas and to introduce him to those who could help him with his important assignment. Now Frank Quinn is the most accommodating man in the world and will go all-out to further the interests of Texas and her scenic parks, but there is a point beyond which no Texan can be pushed.

When Frank arrived in his car to pick up the cameraman and the equipment, he opened the car trunk to load in the numerous boxes of paraphernalia. He learned right away that the several cameras, the light meter, the altimeter, and the thermometer could not ride in the trunk but must ride on the back seat of the car. That left three men to ride on the front seat, because they were taking along an extra man to hold an umbrella over the turban-clad head of the temperamental photographer. Crammed into the front seat, they drove to San Antonio to see the Alamo, the beautiful missions and other scenes which all Texans love, but the photographer saw nothing worthy of his consideration. When they arrived at the place where they were to spend the first night, they found that the custodian of the umbrella and the cameraman had reservations to share a double room and Mr. Quinn had a single room. The photographer said that it would be impossible for him to sleep in the room with another person, so Frank gave his room to the artist and moved in with the third party and that arrangement was maintained for the rest of the trip.

They drove for days across the enormous state and visited untold numbers of places, but the cameraman saw nothing worth the effort it would take to snap a picture. Finally they landed in the Big Bend Country. Even here, in all the scenic beauty and wonder of a majestic land, the photographer could see nothing to record on his priceless film. He announced that he would like to take a picture of a cattle roundup; so a number of cowboys worked two days gathering cattle to set the scene he wanted.

When the equipment was in place and the man in charge of the umbrella shaded the famous head, the photographer eyed the cattle, the cowboys, and the Texas skies. The cloud formations were not to his liking, so he ordered the cowboys to dismiss the cattle. The lighting was not right to produce a perfect picture. On the third roundup the cowboys' tempers were getting short and Frank Quinn and the man with the umbrella were thinking of committing murder, when one of the cowboys saw a big rattlesnake under a bush and eased the tension by shooting the snake instead of the photographer. This brought the turban-clad one to life. He trained the camera lenses on the dead snake, ordered the man holding the umbrella to click the shutter when he gave the signal, and grabbed a sotol stalk and started clubbing the lifeless reptile. The shutter clicked, recording for the whole world to see the only scene in the great state of Texas which the photographer considered worthwhile—a picture of himself killing a dead rattlesnake. That got Frank Quinn. He took the photographer back to the railroad in Alpine and dismissed him. Later Frank received a letter from the editors of the magazine thanking him for his courtesy. He should have received an award for valor above and beyond the call of duty.

Tule Mountain and Tule Spring get their names from a plant which grows there. *Tule* is a sort of cane which grows around springs and watering places. In the same vicinity is Burro Mesa, so-named because many wild burros roamed there. Also in that region is Maverick Mountain, called that because it stands off by itself like an old maverick steer.

Swinging in toward the Tornillo Flat, the area north of the Chisos takes in Slickrock Mountain, named that because the rocks are smooth or slick; the Paint Gap Hills and Paint Gap, their names derived from their brilliant coloring; and Grapevine Hills, named for no better reason than the fact that wild grapes grew there. East of Grapevine Hills are Tornillo Creek and Tornillo Flat. The twisting course of the creek running through the flat by the same name gives the place one version of its name, that the course of the creek is as twisted as the threads of a screw and *tornillo* is the Spanish word for screw. *Tornillo* is also the name of a shrub which grows in that region and bears a screw-like bean. Its roots are said to be twisted also.

Tornillo Creek and Tornillo Flat are two of the best-known names in the Big Bend Country. Never did anything that looks so flat get so high as the Tornillo Creek on a rampage. Its roaring waters have washed everything down it from horses to theses, and even the United States mails have to wait on the banks of the Tornillo just as everything else, while the creek spends its fury. An Easterner who had gone into the Chisos to enjoy the wonderful climate and beautiful scenery while he finished his master's thesis was on his way out with his masterpiece in a trailer. He drove into the Tornillo when it was out of its banks and lost his car, trailer and thesis, and was lucky to escape with his life.

Southeast of Tornillo Flat are the McKinney Hills, named for Devine and John McKinney who ranched there. The McKinneys discovered some of the richest quicksilver ore and did a great deal of developmental work in the Terlingua district. They deserve a prominent place in the region's quicksilver story.

The highest peak in that range of hills is called Roy's Peak, which came to be called that when the surveying crew was mapping the region and living at the Roy Stillwell ranch. One morning they got up and began putting names on the peaks they had drawn and located, when one of them said, "Let's name this highest peak, Roy's Peak," and that's exactly how come it's called that. Roy was constantly being asked how certain places got their names and for the most part he knew, but he said there need never be any doubt about Roy's Peak.

Fifty-four years later the surveyor confirmed this story as true.

Behind Roy's Peak is a long range of mountains which extends from Dog Canyon on the north to Boquillas on the south. The gap through which Nine Point Draw crosses the south end of Santiago Mountains is known as Dog Canyon and the range of mountains south of that gap is usually called the Del Carmen range because of its color. However, most people, even the old-timers, prefer the name "Dead Horse," which is the name now generally used when speaking of the section of the range which lies between Dog Canyon and the Rio Grande.

Tourists have shown a great deal of interest in the popular legend of "how come Dead Horse" was applied to this portion of the Del Carmen range. It was back in 1881, according to this legend, that Captain C. L. Nevill with four men escorted Powell, Gage and Gano, surveyors, down the Rio Grande on a six-weeks' surveying trip. On the way they sighted several bands of Indians who fled when the Americans landed to attack. They came upon one party of Indians who had a number of horses staked near their camp. Before Captain Nevill could attack, they scattered like quail, leaving the animals. Nevill knew that if he left the horses there, the Indians could use them to raid nearby ranches. He couldn't take them with the surveying party; so he concluded that they should kill the horses. The surveyors had previously lost most of their ammunition when their boats capsized in the Rio Grande rapids and Nevill didn't think it was wise to use the little ammunition he had left to destroy the animals; so he ordered his men to blindfold the horses and knock them in the head with an ax. One tender-hearted ranger refused to obey such an order, declaring that he would walk back to camp first. But his *compadres* carried out the order and killed the nine horses. Since then the place has been known as Dead Horse Canyon.

This legend has been accepted as fact, but Ed Nevill, brother of the famous Ranger Captain Charles Nevill, told us that there was a dead horse in that canyon several years before the above incident took place, and that this same canyon was called Dead Horse Canyon before the killing of the horses which gave it the legendary origin. But Arthur Stiles knew nothing of such a name and none of those at the name-selecting meeting held in 1903 mentioned such a story, so he suggested the name Dead Horse Range or Mountain because his favorite saddle horse fell off a cliff in those mountains while they were surveying and was killed. A study of the early maps tends to substantiate this last version.

The area directly west of the Dead Horse or Del Carmen Range encompasses the eastern portion of the Chisos group made up of Nugent Peak, named for a man who once lived there, and Pummel, which is called that because it looks so much like the pummel of a saddle. Wright Mountain, a peak with an elevation of over six thousand feet, on the east side of the Chisos Mountains about a mile east-southeast of Panther Peak, was named for George M. Wright, founder of the Wildlife Division of the National Park Service. Toll Mountain is flat-topped, with an elevation of about 7,420 feet, about one mile northeast of Emory Peak. It was named for Roger W. Toll, then Superintendent of Yellowstone National Park, who was active in the establishment of Big Bend National Park. Wright and Toll had just completed an official inspection of the then-proposed Big Bend National Park and were traveling together when both were killed in an automobile accident near Deming, New Mexico, following their visit to Big Bend.

Panther Peak was called that because of an incident which happened there. Bud Kimble and Joe Moss, early trail blazers in the Big Bend, were on that mountain peak when a large panther leaped between them. They were so frightened and surprised that they just looked at him until he disappeared. After that, it was referred to as Panther Peak. Many panthers have been seen on that mountain. Today the new Big Bend National Park headquarters are located at the foot of Panther Peak, and much new development will take place there under Mission 66 program. At Panther Junction, a visitor center-administration building is proposed for construction with this visitor center serving the park visitors as an over-all park orientation and information point. They can then visit the other sections of the park with a clearer picture of the natural values of the park.

The high peak behind Panther is called Lost Mine Peak, so-named because there is supposed to be a mine there whose exact location has been lost. The legend of "how come it's called that" grew out of a practice during the early days of the Spanish occupation. A presidio was built at San Vicente and was used by the *conquistadores* as a prison. Daily the guards blindfolded the captive Indians and marched them into the Chisos Mountains to work in the silver mine there. The guards stood in the mouth of the shaft and through a narrow pass could see San Vicente across the Rio Grande. There is a trail which runs from the San Vicente ruins across the foothills of the Chisos, only to become lost somewhere on Lost Mine Peak. Those who search for the lost mine must stand at the doorway of the ruins of the Mission de San Vicente or where, when the sun rises on Easter morning, it will shine through a cleft in the Sierra del Carmen right into the entrance to the mine. By following these directions an early official of Brewster County located Lost Mine Peak, but whether or not he found the lost mine, the man didn't say.

Going toward Marathon after leaving the Chisos, tourists can see a splendid growth of giant yucca or Spanish daggers growing mostly to the right or east of the highway. These giant daggers give three place names to the region, Dagger Mountain, Dagger Flat and Dagger Tank.

About 1914 Bill Lemons, still living in Brewster County, was in the goat business with his father and brother at Dagger Flat. They were camped at Dagger Tank. One day Mr. Lemons left his sons tending goats and went to Marathon for supplies. While there he hired a man to help with the extra duties which come up at kidding time. The man he hired had arrived in Marathon on the freight train—just a tramp. He claimed to be nineteen years old, but was rather small and appeared to be younger. When they reached the Lemons' camp at Dagger Flat Tank, the boy did very little in the way of work. He wanted to lie around camp reading Wild West stories.

One Saturday night Bill and his brother came into camp about dark and started to cook supper. Mr. Lemons was sitting in a chair in front of the tent. Bill's brother was sitting near the door and Bill was leaning over the bread pan making bread for supper. He heard the lock of a Winchester work and looked back just as he saw the hired man fire at him. The bullet struck him in the right side, something like a glancing shot, tore two ribs to pieces and then passed on into his left jaw crushing the bone badly. He said the shock spun him around several times. His brother jumped up and started for the killer and was shot between the eyes. Mr. Lemons' leaning forward to arise from the chair, was shot in the tip of the left shoulder, the bullet passing downwards to or near the heart. Seeing both his brother and father killed and being badly wounded himself and without arms for defense, Bill ran off into the sheltering darkness. He made his way to the Marathon–Boquillas road, which was about five miles west of the camp. He met a couple of Mexican boys who were freighters and they went with him to Monroe Payne's place at Bone Spring.

Monroe was not at home, but two of his sons took Bill in a hack to a cabin north and east of Persimmon Gap. They would not take him any farther as they feared the killer would come to their home and kill their mother and the other children. Bill slept in the cabin that night and next morning started on foot to John Henderson's Ranch and was soon overtaken by Henderson and a friend who were in a wagon. Henderson took him to Marathon, arriving about two o'clock Monday morning, some twenty-eight hours after Bill was wounded. Bill said that he had traveled about thirty miles in an effort to get help and had only one drink of water in all that time. His suffering was terrible. Bill was taken to the hospital in El Paso. When he was put on the train in Marathon, the doctor said he could not live to reach El Paso, but forty years later Bill Lemons was still going strong.

Thinking that he had killed all the Lemons family, the murderer concocted a story about how the Mexicans had attacked them and killed the Lemons. When the killer was disarmed, he was turned over to Roy Stillwell who took him to Marathon. It was dark and Roy was put on guard by a strange premonition that the sneaking, secretive youth planned to kill him. Finally, Roy searched the boy and found a long knife concealed in his boot.

The killer was declared insane and confined in an asylum in his home state, Illinois. He escaped some time later and killed two more men without cause. Then he was captured and executed. Some people in the Big Bend Country believed that the killer had read so many Wild West and murder stories that he believed that he could pull off a big killing and put up a yarn to clear himself, becoming a hero, in his own eyes at least.[8]

The first great gorge you see in the Dead Horse Mountains and to the east of the road is called Devil's Den because it is deep and dark, where no sun can shine, and it is said to be fit only for the dwelling of devils. It is so narrow in places that a man must turn sideways to pass through.

Above Devil's Den, the next gorge or break in the mountains is known as Dog Canyon. It separates that section known as the Santiago Mountains from the Dead Horse Mountains or the Sierra del Carmen range. The legend of why it was called Dog Canyon is told on page 3, but years before it was called that it was called Puerta del Camelos, because the camel caravan passed through there while on its expedition in the Southwest. On Lieutenant Echols' map it is called the Pass of the Camels.

The range of mountains paralleling the road to the west

---

8. The story of this tragedy was told by the late Roy Stillwell and the late Captain E. E. Townsend.

is Santiago Mountain range which you cross at Persimmon Gap, so-named because persimmon trees grow around there. They are not just ordinary little green bushes—they are persimmon trees and if it hadn't been for those trees, there would have been one less cowboy to make history in the Big Bend.

One day Jim Sedberry and Roy Stillwell were riding the range together when they came upon two wild steers near Persimmon Gap. One was a big fellow and he looked awful and the other was a little fellow with an uncertain disposition. Roy knew something about the two steers and knew that the little one was salty. The big one was just big—he wasn't mean; so Roy thought he would be nice to Sedberry and let him catch and tie the big one. Roy started for the little one and Sedberry yelled to Roy, "Let me have the little one and you take the big one." Roy said "O.K." But he knew that Sedberry was going to catch hell.

Roy went ahead and tied his big old steer without any trouble and then he started looking for Sedberry. He saw Sedberry's horse running off without a rider in one direction and the little steer running in another direction with a rope around its neck. But he couldn't see Sedberry any place. Finally Sedberry came out from behind a little persimmon bush where he had been hiding. He didn't have any of his shirt on except the collar and the front strip to which the buttons were sewn. The little steer had got up after Sedberry had thrown him, and hooked all the cowboy's clothes off. Sedberry was plenty mad and bawled Roy out for letting him rope the little steer. It was a comical sight to watch Jim running around without his shirt and wailing, "Why did you let me do it, Roy? Why did you let me do it?"

The Comanches used to travel through Persimmon Gap on their raids into Mexico. "Each year, in the light of the Mexican moon—for so they came to term the September full moon—the Comanche War Trail swarmed with parties of these barbaric warriors in troops of half dozen to a hundred or more, including outlaws from many other tribes and even renegades from Mexico, who hurried forward to the carnival of bloodshed and rapine on the south side of the Rio Grande."[9]

Some time in November or December, these raiding parties returned from Mexico bringing with them cattle, captives and horses. When they were pursued they set great prairie fires which stopped the pursuers for a time, while the raiding party deflected from the main trail.

"But there was no way to cover or hide the Great Trail itself. It was worn deep by the hoofs of countless travelers, man and beast, and was whitened by the bones of many animals. It was a great chalk line on the map of West Texas, cutting through the heart of the Big Bend."[10]

A marker at Persimmon Gap locates the place where this Comanche Trail passed through the gap. For many years Cooper's Store at this gap was the clearing house for information from the railroad to the river and travelers going in either direction always stopped to find out what had happened ahead of them. Cooper's Store is no longer there, for the owners sold out to the National Park Service and a Park Ranger Station now occupies that site.

Between Persimmon Gap and Santiago Peak is Muskhog Gap which was named by Joseph Gus Rountree II when he was about eighteen years old and was staying at a ranch called Bone Spring Ranch, owned by his grandfather, John Stillwell. One day Gus was roaming horseback over his grandfather's ranch and he came to a big gap in the mountain range. There he rode right into a herd of Javelina or muskhogs. He saw a baby pig lie down on the open ground and pretend to be dead. Gus rode up to the little pig, leaned over and picked it up without getting off his horse. The pig began

---

9. Carl Graham Raht, *The Romance of Davis Mountains and Big Bend Country,* El Paso, Texas, p. 63. From writings of O. W. Williams.

10. Carl Graham Raht, *The Romance of Davis Mountains and Big Bend Country,* p. 64.

to squeal and struggle. The whole herd charged Gus and his horse. Gus held on to the pig and made a run for it. He took his prize home to his grandfather who immediately turned the pig loose and asked Gus where he got it. Gus told him that he caught the pig in Muskhog Gap because he didn't know any other name to apply to the place where he had captured the pig. Since then it has been called Muskhog Gap because all those on the ranch called it that for years and finally the name stuck.[11]

---

11. The account of the naming of this place was told in a letter written by Mr. Joseph Gus Rountree II to Hallie Stillwell.

Chapter 4

PLACE NAMES ON THE OTHER SIDE OF THE FENCE

GOING OUT of the Chisos toward Marathon, after you cross the Tornillo, to your left are the brilliantly colored Rosillos Mountains (just outside the Park) which derive their name from the Spanish word *rosillos* meaning red or roan, the color of the rocks in the region. Some old maps carry the name Rocio, which is the Spanish word for dew, and some spell the word Rocillos.

On up the road, you pass through Bone Spring Draw which heads at Bone Spring outside the park. This spring and draw came by their names because of the many, many bleached bones scattered about. Two versions of the story tell how those bones came to be there. One relates that there was once a seep spring there in which the cattle bogged down and died trying to reach water. The other story is that animals being driven over the trail were often weakened by long trailing in the desert dust and the spring was the logical stopping place for cattle on the move. Those too weak to go on were left to die. At any rate, those bones gave a name to the place.

Although the following account of what took place at Bone Spring in the early days has nothing to do with the naming of the place, for it was already named when this incident happened, it will be something to remember when you see the draw and it does explain how some of those bones came to be there.

Many colorful characters have stopped to water their horses and to rest at Bone Spring. As late as 1936, an old man arrived in the Big Bend inquiring how to get to Bone Spring. The man was about eighty-eight years old and had a map of

Brewster County marked with a trail leading from Boquillas, Mexico, to Bone Spring. For days he dug in that vicinity, hoping to find the silver bullion which had been buried there years before. Finally he came out with the story that he was the youngest member of Quantrill's Raiders and that Quantrill had drawn the map for him, telling him that years before the young scout had joined the gang, the Raiders had robbed the mines beyond Boquillas, Mexico, and had headed for Texas. They camped at Bone Spring. The men were all sick with typhoid and the horses and wagons were worn-out. They stayed at Bone Spring three or four weeks and it looked as if the men would all die, but only one man finally gave up the ghost. He was buried along with the loot near Bone Spring. The men and teams had become too weak to carry the bullion. No one ever went back for the silver. Some of the bones which bleached on the flats near the spring were those of Quantrill Raiders' horses.

In the 1890's, John Stillwell dug out a watering place at Bone Spring and charged five cents a head for the freighters' mules to water and rest there. Since this was the only watering place between Tornillo and Maravillas Creek in those days, the freighters who hauled ore from Boquillas to Marathon were glad to have a place where their mules could be watered and rested and they could meet their friends in passing. There was a lot of freighting traffic over that road then, and the long burro and mule trains hauling the ore were colorful sights.

Maravillas Creek only runs when it rains and it drains a tremendous territory. Its name comes from the Spanish word *maravilla,* meaning wonder or from the Spanish verb *maravillar,* meaning to be astonished or to wonder. No doubt the first man to name the creek was astonished to find water running in such a desert land.

It was in 1900 that David S. Combs established his ranch on the Maravillas Creek. The ranch was made up of state land which could be homesteaded or leased. Some railroad land adjoining the Combs' ranch came on the market and 32,000 acres were offered to them at $1.60 per acre. The Combs tried to beat the price down to $1.25 per acre, but Col. C. C. Gibbs of San Antonio who handled the sale wouldn't cut it one penny.

Railroad holdings in Brewster and other West Texas counties were numerous, so Colonel Gibbs made a trip in a buckboard to investigate. He went from Alpine to Terlingua and back through Del Norte Gap.

In the meantime showers had fallen in the Marathon country and overflows down the Maravillas had improved the looks of all plant growth. Unfortunately for Combs, Will Wilson had homesteaded on Del Norte Flat and had planted three or four acres in sorghum (cane) and it was beautiful. The road ran right by the little field. Colonel Gibbs was hot and dry when he passed, but he saw the green field, so he drove on down the Maravillas and camped a half-mile below the Combs' house and when Mr. Combs went down to see him, he found the Colonel sitting on the bank of the Creek with his shoes off, dabbling his feet in the cool water of the Maravillas. The price of the land went up to $2.00 an acre immediately and the Combs bought at that price. Mr. Guy Combs always said that Will Wilson's cane cost them $2,000 to $3,000 per ton, which Mr. Combs believes to be a record price for feed.

The story of how Santiago Peak came by its name was told years ago to O. W. Williams by his chainman, Natividad Lujan, when Mr. Williams was surveying in the Big Bend Country. According to legend, Natividad's uncle, Santiago, was killed in a battle with the Apaches when he tried to recover some horses which the Apaches had stolen. He was buried at the foot of the highest peak in the range of mountains and both the peak and the mountain range and a draw paralleling the range of mountains came to be called Santiago after that incident.

A few old Indian fighters who live along the Rio Grande say that the Santiago Range was named for Don Santiago, chief of the Chisos Indians. Perhaps this is true, for it is a matter of record that General Juan de Retana fought an all-day battle with Don Santiago who finally surrendered after losing a number of his followers.

Though it has nothing to do with the naming of the place, it is interesting to note that laid out on the very top of Santiago Peak is the townsite of Progress City. Of course the town was never built, but on the third of January in 1910 a map of the townsite was filed for record in the County Clerk's office in Brewster County. There it is today for anybody to see in the front of Deed Record Volume 17, page 1.

Literally thousands of lots were sold and not all for the same price. The price depended on the sucker. The town was divided into 6,400 lots and on the tip-top of Santiago Peak a large block was reserved for the city hall. Progress City was only a phantom town with lots of no more than twelve feet in width being sold to people who had never heard of the Big Bend Country. Certainly no one ever made use of his property, for the peak was accessible mostly to eagles and wild burros.

Bob Cartledge told this story to Sam Woolford to illustrate the kind of land deals that happened in the Big Bend country.

"One time he was on a Pullman car of the Southern Pacific and this also was back in the old days. Van Sickle of Alpine was in the same compartment. The two Big Bend men were returning from a trip to San Antonio. As the familiar skyline of the Big Bend showed up to the south, the beveled summit of Santiago Peak, they started talking about their part of Texas.

"Across from them sat a traveler who kept one ear cocked to their conversation. Finally he crossed the aisle and said, 'Gentlemen, I've been listening to you talk, and I can see that you're familiar with this area. I have a town lot near Alpine and I'm considering stopping over to look up my property.'

"Van Sickle knew a great deal about the location of various tracts of land in the Big Bend so when the stranger drew a deed out of his suitcase, the judge studied it carefully before speaking. At last he shook his head, sighed, and turned to the stranger.

" 'My friend, do you see that flat-topped mountain about 40 miles south of here?'

"The other answered, 'I can barely see it.'

"Van Sickle continued: 'Well, my friend, your town lot is right on top of that mountain. And there hasn't been anybody up there since the rangers ran the Apaches off that mountain-top back in the 1870's.' "[1]

When Captain C. D. Wood was county judge, it was discovered that no taxes were being paid on any of the lots on Santiago Peak and it was costing hundreds of dollars every year to enter all the lots on the unrendered roll. Therefore the whole works were expunged from the tax records.

On the road toward Marathon, to the east of Highway 227, is a mountain known today as Horse Mountain, but it is easy to see that it should be called Camel's Hump, since a camel kneeling with his head on the ground can be seen without stretching the imagination. In 1859, the Camel Caravan under the leadership of Lieutenants Hartz and Echols passed that way and pitched camp there after a long journey made through the Southwest in an experiment testing the capabilities of the camel as compared with the efficiency of the mule. The leaders of this expedition gave the mountain its name—Camel Hump. Just when the people of the region began to call it Horse Mountain, no one seems to know. A study of the old maps of this region shows that there have been a number of changes in the place names. It is hoped that when the U.S. Board on Geographic Names finally passes on the names in this region that there will be no more changes.

Fort Peña Colorado was established as a sub-post of Fort Davis when the Indians had become so destructive in that region in the 1870's. But when the railroad was built across the Big Bend in 1882, the families abandoned the fort to

---

1. Sam Woolford, "Tales of the Big Bend," San Antonio *Light*, March 27, 1955, p. 19A.

move to Marathon, which was being built along the railroad. About 1893, the soldiers abandoned the Fort which had adopted its name from the colored rocks in that region. *Peña Colorado* is Spanish for colored rock.

The site of the old military camp is now a part of the Combs Cattle Company, one of the largest ranches in Brewster County. A part of the post land was given by the owners to the citizens of Brewster County for a park and playground. A nice swimming pool, barbecue pits, tables, dance platform, and huge shade trees make this one of the most inviting spots in West Texas. Annually, on the Fourth of July, the citizens of Marathon give a big barbecue and dance at Old Fort Peña Colorado, and hundreds of people come to enjoy the hospitality of the Marathon residents. This public park is about four and a half miles southwest of Marathon.

Just out of the Big Bend National Park boundary to the south and east, but still within the Big Bend area are located several places of historical value and importance. Very little has been written about this section of the Big Bend Country, for it has never been connected with the outside by roads and trails that strangers care to travel, yet in the early days quite a few people lived here.

Below Boquillas Canyon is Telephone Canyon, named that because during World War I a telephone line was put across the Del Carmen into the canyon where a small detachment of soldiers was stationed. Running up Ernst Valley is Strawhouse Trail which leads, appropriately enough, to a straw house. When and by whom it was built, no one knows. But the straw house gave the trail its name.

Just below Telephone Canyon is Stillwell Canyon, which joins the Rio Grande at Stillwell Crossing. This canyon and crossing get their names from the Stillwell family, who were among the first pioneers of the Big Bend. The first Stillwell made a trip into Mexico with the Mormons in the 1870's and there he was robbed of everything he had: money, horses, and wagon. He had nothing but his pocketknife to live by and with that knife he butchered rattlesnakes and ate them. In that way he survived until he could walk out of Mexico. But that didn't keep him from returning there to ranch, and in the early 1880's the Stillwells were ranching in Mexico at Huerfanito, chief watering place on the old Piedra Blanca Ranch in northern Coahuila and around Pico Etereo. They built a boat or raft and kept it at Stillwell Crossing for all to use.

In those days the Rio Grande was indeed a grand river, its waters deep and wide. One just didn't ride or wade across it, he swam or crossed in a boat. The Stillwells were doing much of their trading at Marathon at that time, and the boat was very useful. The supplies were loaded into the boat, and by rowing and swimming his horse behind the boat, a man could negotiate the crossing.[2]

Many herds of cattle crossed at Stillwell Crossing, herds from Mexico to Texas and herds from Texas to Mexico. The Stillwell boys, John, Joe, Will, Roy and Charlie, with their sister, Alice and her husband W. T. Henderson, were at that time the life of this section. They were not unlike Don Milton Faver who ranched on the Chihuahua Trail and whose ranch house was a fort. Don Milton made his own treaties with Indians and controlled the area around Shafter. In the area around Stillwell Crossing, the Stillwells were in control. Their only competition was from their Mexican neighbors. Like any other place in the world, some neighbors were good and some were bad. The stories of the Stillwells' fight with the bad ones made history in the Big Bend Country, and it lasted for quite a spell.

In 1890, while the Stillwells were living at the Carmen Ranch, named for the Del Carmen Mountains in northern Coahuila, Mexico, their son, Roy, took typhoid fever and for

2. The 1880-90 maps of the Big Bend region show very few names, but Stillwell Crossing; Stillwell Trail, leading toward the settlements being built along the railroad; and Stillwell Canyon show that the Stillwells were the first to really know that frontier. Later maps show the Stillwell ranches in Texas, Stillwell Mountain, and Roy's Peak.

weeks his young life hung by no more than a fevered breath. His father sent for the Mexican doctor who lived at the silver mines. He was a good doctor and with the help of Nellie, Roy's sister, who nursed and cared for him, the boy recovered. Exhausted by the trial of waiting on her sick brother, Nellie took the fever and lacked the vitality to survive. She was buried at Stillwell Crossing on the Texas side. Her grave is still there.

Just north of Stillwell Canyon is Stairway Peak and Stairway Mountain, so-named because the mountain looks like a stairway when viewed from a distance. One of the largest land suits in the state of Texas was fought over a lost survey corner in the area of Stairway Mountain. Surveyor Gano, with E. L. Gage and Joe Irving, had made a trip down the Rio Grande surveying and establishing corners in blocks of land. Gano established the original southwest corner for Block G-1 back in 1881. Later on, every surveyor who tried to find that corner failed. Since it was never located, the whole countryside was thrown for a loop for years to come. Finally a lawsuit grew out of a controversy over that corner and a corner was established by the courts. But the original corner and monument are still lost and just as illusive as are the gold mines in the Big Bend.

Another canyon in this area is Heath Canyon, named for Tom Heath who came to the Big Bend along with Hubert Wigzell. They were both Englishmen. The two men built a large water tank and a little house nearby which was painted red, causing the tank to be called Red House Tank. The house is no longer there but the tank is, and it still goes by that name. Tom Heath lived on the Rio Grande in the beautiful canyon which bears his name. Hubert Wigzell settled about twenty-five miles north where the Maravillas Creek cuts through the mountains for fifteen miles forming a canyon known as the "Shut-Up," so-called because the canyon is closed in by mountains. "Shut-up" is a term used by topographers in describing such contours as this. Heath Creek, also named for Tom Heath, crosses into the park area.

Black Gap, so-named because the rocks are black and look like iron, is now the headquarters for the State Game Preserve called Black Gap Game Management Area, but it is known locally as Black Gap.

Stillwell Mountain, named for Roy Stillwell, joins Black Gap on the north and is also covered by black rocks. Cupola, or Sugar Loaf Peak, is a high peak east of Black Gap. It was named for its appearance.

Dove Mountain, which lies northward from Cupola Peak, once had a spring on it where many doves came for water. The spring dried up in the early 1900's and has never had any water since. The cowboys always thought that the big earthquake in San Francisco caused the spring to dry up. Mr. Jim P. Wilson, ranching over in Green Valley, had one of his water wells to go dry right after the San Francisco quake. It never did produce water again.

On down from Dove Mountain and Cupola Mountain, there is a canyon called Mouth of the Maravillas where the creek runs into the Rio Grande, though the canyon has widened as it approaches the river to the extent that it is almost imperceptible. This junction of the Maravillas and the Rio Grande is sometimes called the Maravillas Crossing or the Paso de los Ladrones (Spanish for Ford or Pass of the Robbers). Three train robbers who robbed the Southern Pacific in the late 1890's used this crossing while being trailed by the law in and out of Mexico. Big Benders say that the Mouth of the Maravillas is "the fartherest away from nowhere of any place on earth." When you get there, let us know what you think!

One of the most important canyons in legend and story of the Big Bend Country is Reagan Canyon, named for the four Reagan brothers, John, Jim, Frank, and Lee. About 1884, the Reagan brothers were ranching in this area. They had a Seminole by the name of Bill Kelly working for them. One day they sent Bill across the river into Mexico to hunt some horses. Bill didn't find the horses but he did find a chunk of gold ore. The Reagans didn't believe Bill when he said he had found gold and cussed him out for not finding the horses. In a few days Bill left the Reagan brothers and went to Mexico City with a trainload of cattle. In the meantime he stopped with the Stillwells at their ranch in Mexico and showed them his gold. And it was with John Stillwell and the cattle that he went to Mexico City. Before he ran away from the Reagans and went to the Stillwells, Bill had become acquainted with the train conductor by the name of Lock Campbell and had told him about the gold. Mr. Campbell took the gold samples and had them assayed. The result of the assay was amazing—something like $80,000 a ton. Then Bill Kelly disappeared. Lock Campbell searched for the gold mine and he searched for Bill. The Reagans spent a fortune looking for the mine. Others joined in the search. One man looked for the Lost Nigger Mine for seventeen years. There has scarcely been a day since 1884 that someone has not been looking for that mine, but no one has stumbled across it yet. Big Benders often wonder what effect it would have had on the region had Lee Reagan said to Bill Kelly back in 1884, "Damn the horses. Lead me to that gold mine!" instead of "Damn your gold. I sent you to hunt horses!"

In this area of the Big Bend Country there are several places bearing the name of Bullis. Bullis Trail runs through Bullis Gap in the Bullis Gap Range in the southeastern part of Brewster County to Bullis Crossing on the Rio Grande, about one hundred miles above the mouth of the Pecos.

The name of Bullis is an honored one in the Big Bend Country, and a brief summary of the story of the man whose name is applied to the places mentioned above should be told here so that those who may have forgotten the services he rendered the people of the frontier will think of him as they explore this region, and tourists who may not have heard about his gallantry may know something of what lies behind the place names. In an old clipping in the Bullis family files, there appeared this statement:

ROOSEVELT COMMENDED GENERAL BULLIS

One of Most Noted Indian Fighters in Army Won 100 Frontier Battles

---

Known as "The Thunderbolt," and "The Whirlwind" to tribes in Texas and Mexico, Brigadier General John Lapham Bullis was one of the most famous Indian fighters of all American history. His name has been honored in many ways, but perhaps most permanently by the establishment of Camp Bullis north of San Antonio.

From 1870 until 1882 General Bullis was active in campaigns that removed depredating Indians from Texas soil forever. He fought in some of the most vigorous Indian campaigns on Texas soil, and, as became a man of his reputation, he participated in the final campaign against a raiding tribe and aided in closing that chapter of Texas History.

General Bullis was, perhaps, the most loved Indian fighter in history. His courage and gallantry, and laudable successes, won for him distinction accorded to few Army men. The people of West Texas presented him with a gold sword which probably has no equal.—

The Congress of the United States recommended him to the President for promotion, and he was honored publicly upon many occasions. In the records of the War Department are many citations of his bravery and good judgment as a soldier and commander. He lived in Texas for nearly forty years, and is recognized by historical writers as "the greatest Indian fighter the Army ever produced."

> *He demanded no hardship or risk of his men, that he did not share, and due to his indomitable courage the scourge of murder and arson that reigned in Texas outpost settlements after the Civil War, was ended.*

Colonel Martin L. Crimmins, in writing about John L. Bullis in *The Army and Navy Courier,* November, 1926, described the famous sword which had been presented to the great Indian fighter in 1881. "It is certainly the finest sword ever presented in this part of the country to a military hero. The sword was made by the famous firm of Bent & Bus, of Boston. The hilt and scabbard is fire-gilded and most elaborately and appropriately ornamented and inscribed. The hilt is the Goddess of Liberty and the American Eagle combined. The guard is illustrated with a camp scene in the Chinati Mountains; then follows the inscription 'Bullis, the friend of the frontier.' A monogram, and a representation of the warrior himself; then another inscription, 'He protected our homes—our homes are open to him.' Then lengthwise on the scabbord, 'Presented to Jno. L. Bullis by the people of Western Texas.' "

In *The Century Magazine,* July, 1889, Frederick Remington had this to say about Captain Bullis of the Twenty-fourth Infantry. "If the deeds of this officer had been done on civilized battle fields instead of in silently leading a pack of savages over the desert waste of the Rio Grande or the Staked Plain, they would have gotten him his niche in the temple of fame. Alas! They are locked up in the gossip of the army mess-room, and end in the soldiers' matter-of-fact joke about how Bullis used to eat his provisions in the field, opening one can a day from the packs, and whether it was peaches or corned-beef, making it suffice. The Indians regard him as almost supernatural, and speak of the 'Whirlwind' with many grunts of admiration as they narrate his wonderful achievements."

It is believed that this article was read by Theodore Roosevelt, for he and Remington were friends and when Roosevelt hunted peccaries in Southwest Texas he must have heard of Bullis who was the hero of that region and whose name was a household word. So it was that when President Roosevelt came into office he looked with favor on men like Bullis and Pershing. Major Bullis was appointed Brigadier General on May 24, 1904, and on May 26, 1911, he died in San Antonio, Texas, at the age of seventy.

Colonel Crimmins said that the Indians along the Rio Grande called General Bullis the "Thunderbolt" because they never knew when he was coming and when he did come he arrived with the force of a whirlwind. Certainly, few names in the Big Bend Country have a more illustrious background than does that of Bullis.

San Francisco Creek runs into the Rio Grande near the foot of Bullis Gap Mountains. It is said that the creek was named for the Franciscan Fathers who traveled along its course on their missions in the region.

Chapter 5

PLACE NAMES WEST OF THE PARK AND ALONG HIGHWAY 118

L*EAVING* the west entrance to the Big Bend National Park on the Study Butte–Alpine road, it is likely that you will notice Maverick Mountain which lies to the right and northeast of the road. It is so named because it stands alone, apart from any other physical feature. This entrance is known as the Maverick Mountain Entrance to the park because of the nearby mountain.

Don't fail to stop and get acquainted with Study Butte (pronounced Stew-dy), one of the old landmarks in the Big Bend. It was named for Will Study who lived there during the time the quicksilver mines were being developed. About 1917, W. D. and Rubye Burcham moved to Study Butte, and for the next twenty-five years were prominently associated with the quicksilver industry—most of those years being spent in Study Butte. W. D. Burcham is one of the best authorities on the Big Bend quicksilver industry, for as things happened, he recorded them and he was always able to write objectively.

A few miles from Study Butte on Highway 118 going toward Alpine, one of the formations which attracts tourists is the honeycombed surface of Bee Mountain named for the hives of bees which live in the crevices. So numerous are these bee caves that the whole mountain resembles an enormous beehive.

In Bee Cave Canyon was found one of the largest Indian shelters in the region. It is over a thousand feet long with a maximum overhang of one hundred feet. Evidences of Basket Maker and earlier Indian cultures have been found there.

Directly west of Bee Mountain there is a large stone corral which was built between 1884 and 1886 under the direction of Captain James B. Gillett, at that time the manager of the G-4 outfit. The Mexicans used to call it Las Tapias and the cowboys called it the Lower Rock Pens, but it is on the map as Rock Corral. Old Magarito (Maggie) Deanda helped build the rock corral, and in 1937 he still loved to tell about the work he did for Captain Gillett. He was then about seventy-seven years old.

On the map of the Big Bend Country there are several places designated as Rock Corral and most of them have interesting histories and were built in the early days. There is one such corral on the trail which runs by Contrabando Mountain, far to the southwest of the one built by old Maggie Deanda.

In the area of Bee Mountain is Wild Horse Mountain, so-named because a band of wild horses roamed there for years. Then there is Willow Spring, marked by a growth of willow trees which gives both the spring and mountain their names. Willow Mountain is a volcanic, columnar wall rising over a thousand feet above the valley floor. The rock formation which forms the side of the mountain resembles thousands of willow poles standing on end. After a rain the top of the mountain greens up until it looks very much like the top of an enormous tree.

On up the road where mountains surround a desert-like valley are the Christmas Mountains, the Corazones and Egg Shell or Hen Egg Mountain, all three of which are named for their unusual shapes. There are two versions to the story of "how come the Christmas Mountains are called that." One is that from a distance their numerous pointed peaks look very much like a growth of Christmas trees, and the other version describes a family which went into those mountains to camp for the summer and didn't emerge until Christmas. Corazones Mountain gets its name from its heart shape, *corazon* being the Spanish word for heart. Hen Egg or Egg Shell (it goes by both names) was named for its egg-like appearance.

The Agua Fria Mountain, Spring and Creek all get their names from the Spanish words *agua fria,* meaning cold water. Agua Fria Spring flows from the base of a six-hundred-foot cliff. The spring was once the site of an extensive Indian camp. The cliff which overhangs the spring is covered with pictographs, some of which are very odd and interesting and tell the story of Indian activity in the region.

The Agua Fria runs into the Alamo Cesario Creek which, according to Indian legend, got its name in this way: A band of Mescalero Apaches had been on a raid into Mexico where they captured a Mexican girl named Cesaria. They carried her to their camp at Agua Fria. While unloading their plunder, they tied their captive to a cottonwood tree which the Mexicans call *alamo.* Friends and relatives of the girl had followed the trail and soon made an attack on the Indians. The Indians were driven away and the girl rescued. So the cottonwood tree to which the girl had been tied was called *Alamo Cesaria* or Cesaria's Cottonwood. In time this name was fastened to the locality.

According to the late Henry Fletcher,[1] prominent local rancher, Nine Point Mesa has nine projecting points which lends the place its name, but around Marathon the tale has circulated for years that the mountain is called that because someone killed a nine-point buck up on top of the mesa and he always referred to the place "where I killed that nine-point buck," until finally the mesa name was shortened to Nine Point. No doubt it is a misnomer, but it had plenty of meaning to the man who named it and, as was pointed out in the beginning of this book, at the time most of these places were named, no one had any idea he would ever be trying to explain how come he called it that.

---

1. The late Henry Fletcher was also historian for the Highland Hereford Association and did much research on place names in the Big Bend. The Governor of Texas appointed a committee to select names for places in the Big Bend Park area. Serving on this committee were Henry Fletcher, Mrs. Roy Stillwell, Dr. Clifford B. Casey of Sul Ross College, and Mrs. W. T. Burnham.

About halfway from Study Butte to Alpine, is a hill called Butcherknife Hill. It is the place where stagecoaches used to stop. Once a man traveling south lost a butcher knife at the spring in the foothills of this mountain. After that he always referred to the spring as "the place where I lost the butcher knife." A few weeks later a man traveling north found the butcher knife and he began referring to the spring as "the place where I found the butcher knife." So it was that in both the north and south ends of Brewster County the place became known as Butcherknife Spring. The mountain became known by the same name as is so often the case of places in the Big Bend.

Mitchell Mesa was named for a prominent Marfa family of that name who ranched there a number of years ago. On toward Alpine is Elephant Mountain which is so-named because of its shape and size. So large is it on top that, according to Nevill Haynes, he can run two hundred head of heifers up there in normal times. It is good grassy ranch land with plenty of water and he drives two hundred young heifers up there and leaves them for two years or until they are of breeding age.

A creek that drains a lot of country in this vicinity is called Calamity. Once a flood melted down an adobe house on the Nevill ranch and some people were drowned there. It is claimed that the first person to view the disaster exclaimed, "Oh, what a calamity," thus christening the creek.

On June 27, 1955, a tornado and flash flood struck the Lee Kokernot ranch where Hallie Stillwell was pasturing her cattle because she had been "droughted" out on the Stillwell ranch. She watched the dark cloud hovering over the Big Bend and hoped she would get rain. The next day she got the news. Most of her cattle had been drowned in Chalk Draw, a tributary to Calamity Creek. For years Hallie Stillwell had worked on this book about the stories behind the place names in the Big Bend Country, and it seemed like cruel irony that she had to add a footnote to her story. A number of her cattle had washed all the way down Chalk Draw and were found in Calamity Creek.

The last group of mountains of particular interest and which can be seen from Highway 118 as you travel toward Alpine is made up of Cienega Mountain, Cathedral Mountain, and Mt. Ord. Cienega gets its name from the Spanish word meaning marsh. Legend has it that friendly Indians directed Lawrence Haley to the Valle de los Cienegas (Valley of the Marshes).

Cathedral Mountain is called that because it looks like a cathedral. The highest point on Cathedral Mountain is Haley's Peak, named for Lawrence Haley who ranched there in the 1880's.

Barry Scobee told us this story and when you look up at Haley's Peak, it is likely that you will remember this account of Lawrence Haley and those to whom he left his ranch.

"Bob Slight was the first man I ever met in Alpine. He lived in London and it was there that he saw Buffalo Bill's show and after that he took American fever and landed in Galveston. Somehow he got to the Big Bend and went to herding sheep for Lawrence Haley. He stayed with Haley for many years. And George Brown, an Australian, was with Haley, too. Bob Slight told me that Brown was alone with Haley when Haley died, there on Cathedral Peak ranch. Toward the end, in the cricket-still night, Haley directed Brown to give Bob some of the cattle. Brown gave him money, or cattle, to the tune of $40,000 worth. Later I asked Brown why he did it. 'Nobody heard Haley ask you to,' I commented. 'It was the right thing to do,' Brown said. I never saw Haley, but I talked with people not long after his death. W. B. Hancock told me he was at the funeral. 'I just stood there and looked at George Brown, thinking he was not a Texas cowman, and wondering what he'd do with that fine ranch of Haley's with its good fences with posts every sixteen feet and staves in between.' "

The ranch is still owned by the Brown family. Mr. and

Mrs. DeBarbrie have reopened the Lodge which was once operated by Pete Crawford, a former Texas Ranger. The old barn that houses the recreation room of the Lodge was built about seventy years ago and the nails used in its construction were square and forged there on the ranch. Cathedral Mountain Lodge is one of the most popular places in the region to go for good steak dinners, honest-to-goodness barbecue or any other food a customer might want. The guest rooms are decorated in keeping with the surroundings, and when guests ask questions about the region's past, the DeBarbries can answer them, for Mrs. DeBarbrie is a daughter of George A. Brown, and her husband has studied the history of the area carefully and has learned the story of Lawrence Haley's ranch from every source available.

Going into the park or coming out of the park by way of Highway 118, it is worth the time it takes to go to the Cathedral Mountain Lodge for a meal and a stroll around just to see for yourself what it was that drew Lawrence Haley to that spot seventy-five years ago.

The last high mountain on the right of the road going toward Alpine from Study Butte is Ord Mountain, named for General E. O. C. Ord who was an Indian fighter and Commander of the Department of Texas about 1877. It was once called Del Norte Mountain.

Alpine comes into view when you top out on the Big Hill, so-dubbed because it is just exactly that—a Big Hill.

Most famous landmark in Langtry, Texas. *Benton S. Cooper.*

Amon G. Carter – Mr. Texas.
Rhea-Engert.

The center of Big Bend National Park is dominated by the Chisos Mountains which rise over 7,500 feet above sea level. They are formed of igneous rocks which were molten millions of years ago. In some places, the molten material breeched the surface and flowed as great sheets of lava. In other places, great molten domes cooled and solidified beneath the surface and were later exposed by erosion. Visitors to Big Bend National Park can drive up into the Chisos Mountains on a good surfaced road maintained by the National Park Service, United States Department of the Interior. *U.S. Department of the Interior, National Park Service.*

Ranger Rod Broyles on patrol at Boquillas Canyon. *National Park Service.*

Boot Canyon, showing the rock like an inverted boot, which gives the canyon its name. Crown Mountain is beyond. *Department of the Interior.*

Horseback riding on South Rim Trail in Big Bend National Park. *Texas Highway Department.*

Boquillas, Mexico, as seen from Big Bend National Park. *W. Ray Scott, National Park Concessions, Inc.*

Lon Garrison, former Big Bend National Park Superintendent, looking through field glasses while on a Park Service exploratory trip. The party is about one-third of the way through Boquillas Canyon from Boquillas. The Del Carmen Mountains in the background form an east wall of the canyon and rise 5000 feet above the Rio Grande. *Glenn Burgess.*

In the distance, framed by the arch of this Big Bend roadway tunnel, is the high ridge of the Sierra Del Carmen range in Mexico. The prominent point in the center is called Shot Tower. *Hunter's.*

Rio Grande as seen from Camino del Rio. The scenic river road was opened in November, 1961. Running from Presidio to the Big Bend National Park, it gives a third entrance to the park. *Hunter's.*

The Mule Ear Peaks as seen from the head of Joe's Creek. *Department of the Interior.*

Castolon store and gas station, Big Bend National Park. *National Park Concessions, Inc.*

Terlingua, Texas, the site of the great quicksilver mines. The late Howard E. Perry's house is at the extreme right. *Glenn Burgess.*

Curved bridge span Tornillo Creek. *National Park Service.*

These giant daggers give three place names to the region — Dagger Flat, Dagger Mountain, and Dagger Flat Tank. *W. D. Smithers.*

The Chisos Basin from Panther Pass. The spectacular target in the gunsight of the window is Carter Peak. *Peter Koch.*

Sunday afternoon at Lajitas on the banks of the Rio Grande. *Glenn Burgess.*

Mrs. Lyndon B. Johnson, wearing a cowgirl hat, accepts a painting called "Treasure Mountain" from Mrs. Hallie Stillwell. The painting by Pauline Law of New York was given to Mrs. Johnson by the women of Alpine as a memento of her visit to Big Bend National Park. Members of a band from El Paso stand in the background. Secretary of the Interior, Stewart Udall, stands at left. *W. Ray Scott, National Park Concessions, Inc.*

Chapter 6

DOWN THE TRACKS —HEADING WEST

L*ANGTRY* is the eastern railway entrance into the region known as the Big Bend Country. West of Langtry, the Rio Grande is seen from the train for the last time until it reaches a point just out of El Paso, for the railroad cuts across the northern boundary of the Rio Grande's big bend. Some of the most colorful history of the region centers around the construction of the Southern Pacific lines when the construction engineers, the laborers, and those who came to guard the building of the iron-railed road against the opposition of the Indians collided head on with that frontiersman Judge Roy Bean—Law West of the Pecos.

The canyon of the Pecos presented real difficulties to construction crews building toward the time and place when the eastern and western segments of the Southern Pacific would meet. The engineers building toward the west decided to turn south to the edge of the Rio Grande, cross the Pecos there on an ordinary structure barely above the high water mark and return to open country at a station called Shumla. It was near this station that the connecting link was fastened in place by a gold spike on January 12, 1883, at two o'clock in the afternoon. (Shumla was named for a Turkish fort which was surrounded by hills similar to those found in this location.)

This loop of about twenty-five miles was built at great expense because excavations had to be made in solid rock and two tunnels had to be built. After construction it was found that the rock composing the walls of the canyon is soft limestone, full of seams and fissures. After heavy rains the rock falls made it necessary to patrol the tracks day and night to ensure against accidents. The expense of repairs and watching the line led the company's engineers to seek another route almost immediately after the opening of the road.

On this loop, located near the mouth of the Pecos, was the settlement of Vinegarroon where Roy Bean lived before he moved to Langtry. Mr. Hugh S. Johnson, who spent a part of his youth in a cavalry regiment in this area, says that the story of Roy Bean as the Law West of the Pecos begins at a crossing of the Pecos called Vinegarroon, which Lieutenant Bullis blasted with black gunpowder out of the stubborn rock. A vinegarroon is a large, southwestern whip scorpion which emits a vinegar-like odor when alarmed. Because a lot of these scorpions are found near the place where Roy Bean first held forth, the settlement was called Vinegarroon. And that name, not known to everybody, came in mighty handy for a cowboy from the Big Bend Country who was stationed in the South Pacific during the World War II. He figured he could make a little money on the side selling a potent drink to his buddies. He made his brew from some native grains which he induced the natives to gather for him. One day while he was on K.P. he was cooking up a batch of his brew when the commanding officer made a surprise inspection. A number of vinegar bottles lined up along the wall were already filled with the home brew. The officer sniffed. The cowboy-soldier kept right on stirring his concoction.

"What's in those bottles?" snapped the officer.

"Vinegar, sir."

"What the Hell are you going to use all that vinegar for?"

"Well, sir, I thought I'd cook up a batch of vinegarroon for the boys."

Lest he appear uninformed, the officer didn't ask what vinegarroon was and the Big Bender didn't elaborate. Roy Bean himself couldn't have done better under the circumstances.

Several books have been written on Judge Roy Bean—Law

West of the Pecos—and a television show by that title appears over WABD, Channel 5 in New York City, once a week, spreading his story across the country. The old frontiersman would have loved this publicity, but we wonder if the fiction written about him wouldn't bring down the gavel of the real Roy Bean and call forth, "It ain't so, and by Gobs that's my rulin'." But the current portrayals of the old man serve to keep alive the legend of Roy Bean and those who go to the Big Bend country will know something about the man who lived and worked at Vinegarroon and Langtry.

It was about 1892 that the Pecos High Bridge was built[1] and Roy Bean moved from the abandoned crossing at Vinegarroon to a place near the station called Langtry, named for the construction foreman who handled a gang of Chinese laborers employed to build the road through that section. The popular version of a legend credits the name of this station to the Jersey Island actress, Lily Langtry, with whom Roy Bean was completely smitten. And she did visit the place in the 1890's, but the station was named Langtry before her visit and even before Roy Bean invited her there. The records of the Southern Pacific make this point clear, but Miss Langtry perhaps didn't know that it wasn't named for her—

1. When the Pecos High Bridge was dedicated on June 6, 1923, people in the area thought high water would be no further problem at the old crossing of the Pecos near Langtry, but in June, 1954, the bridge was swept away like a cobweb before a roaring 86-foot wall of water created by a 20-inch rainfall which fell on the Langtry area in a sudden cloudburst. About a year later, construction was started on a new bridge and on April 27, 1957, the new Pecos High Bridge was dedicated. The $1,300,000 structure stands 276 feet above the river and never again will traffic on Highway 90 be disrupted by a rise on the Pecos. With the completion of the proposed ninety-million dollar Diablo Dam Project, water will be backed up in the Rio Grande, Pecos, and Devil's River and the side canyons, but the new bridge will span the lake and give tourists a spectacular view of natural and man-made wonders. If Roy Bean could see the new bridge near his beloved Langtry, no doubt he'd comment, "By Gobs, that's some bridge!"

and Roy Bean's admiration for the actress has been the subject of many a story which adds color to the stark surroundings.

In some of the early stories of this region, the site near Langtry was referred to as Eagle's Nest and there was a perfectly good reason for that name.

"Opposite the village of Langtry, near the top of a vertical cliff some 300 feet high, is a small bluff cavern. Poised on the ledge of this inaccessible cavern is a huge pile of sticks skillfully entwined into what was perhaps one of the largest birds' nest in America. Since the Trans–Pecos country was first known this nest has been a landmark, and until lately had been inhabited by a pair of eagles which here annually brought forth their young. A few years since, however, some soldiers stationed near this place——killed the birds which even the hardened white frontiersmen had long protected."[2]

On April 25, 1875, Eagle's Nest Crossing was the scene of a battle between Lieutenant Bullis and his Seminole Scouts and the Indians. When the Southern Pacific established a grading camp there, they called it Eagle's Nest. Soon a little settlement grew up a short distance from the camp and it was called Langtry to honor the construction foreman who had worked so hard to build the railroad through the difficult terrain.

When Dr. Robert T. Hill and his party completed their exploration of the canyons of the Rio Grande about 1900, they landed upon a little beach opposite the great eagle's nest and sent up to Langtry for a packhorse to carry their belongings to the railway station. It was then that Dr. Hill met Roy Bean, and, from the story he tells of that meeting and the succeeding hours, we get a picture of the legendary Judge that no other writer or personal acquaintance has mentioned.

---

2. Dr. Robert T. Hill, "Running the Canyons of the Rio Grande," Part V, *The Dallas Morning News,* Dallas, Texas, Sept. 16, 1934, p. 17-III.

"We were received by a famous old frontiersman whose hospitable house was decorated with a peculiar sign reading:

LAW WEST OF THE PECOS

ROY BEAN

JUSTICE OF THE PEACE AND
NOTARY PUBLIC

SAN ANTONIO LAGER BEER

"It was under these circumstances that I met this fine old frontiersman with the bark on, who had been so unfairly caricatured in the Dallas courthouse, and whom I met often again in succeeding days and learned to know better.

"We had hardly reached the railway track when we became aware that civilization's dangers are sometimes greater than those of nature. A locomotive whistle was heard in the distance, the first time that sound had greeted our ears for over a month. From the fact that this whistling continued for a long time we inferred that it was a signal of distress and that a Southern Pacific train had become derailed somewhere on the wild and desert prairies to the east of us. Soon the hand car of a section foreman appeared. An appeal for assistance was made and my party with its small first-aid-to-the-injured outfit was conveyed some five miles out into the desert where a huge freight train, pulled by two gigantic locomotives and richly laden with varieties of goods for the Orient, had jumped the track and tumbled into a chaotic pile. Nearly all night long we attended to the injured and the dead.

"Looking at that desolate country in 1900, one would hardly be able to find an inhabitant, except those of the few shacks then in Langtry.

"But when that wreck scattered goods over the prairie, looters began to gather like flies by the scores from apparently nowhere.—bad men both American and Mexican sprang up from nowhere and looted this wreck—all but two, Roy Bean and his son. The former said to his son, 'Son, keep away.' And that is why I loved the old man. There was an inherent sense of honor beneath all of the outer roughness."[3]

At Langtry, visitors often stop to visit the home of Judge Roy Bean who was a duly-elected Justice of the Peace, but the title of Judge was sort of his own idea, as were the decisions which he handed down and made stick with the help of his one law book and a couple of pistols and a firm, "And by Gobs that's my rulin'."

The next station after Langtry of any importance is the non-agency station of Lozier which was named in honor of an Indian chief. The railroad crosses Lozier Canyon several times, because the canyon winds through the region like a snake's trail. Many passengers on the Southern Pacific know what it means to wait for the water to run down in Lozier Canyon or for the tracks to be repaired after the flood waters have done their damage.

Dryden was named for Colonel Dryden, formerly Chief Engineer of the Southern Pacific Railroad. The main line reached Dryden in 1882. It was an early-day shopping center for Big Benders.

Sanderson was named for a railroad foreman and has been a railway terminal since shortly after the opening of the road. Roundhouse facilities were provided there, and in the early 80's Sanderson was the telegraph relay point instead of El Paso. Sanderson has served the ranchmen of that region as a livestock shipping center for many years.

Maxon is named for Lieutenant Thomas Maxon of the U.S. Army, who in 1871, while on patrol duty with troops, discovered the springs at this point and his soldiers named it in honor of their leader. It was first listed on the maps as Maxon Springs. In 1900, the passenger train, now identified as No. 109, was wrecked at a curve near this station. For some unknown reason, the locomotive failed to take the curve and

---

3. Dr. Robert T. Hill, "Running the Canyons of the Rio Grande," p. 17-III.

continued head-on into the country; the entire train, with the exception of a private car on the rear of the train, followed the engine clear of the railroad roadbed, turned turtle and every coach, being of wood construction, burned. As there were a large number of immigrants on the train, the exact number of people who met their deaths in the wreckage was never definitely determined, although estimated to be between forty and fifty. Engineer Al. G. Mast was scalded to death.[4]

Tesnus was originally called Tabor, but because it conflicted with a larger station elsewhere in the state it had to be changed. It is now the word Sunset spelled backward, Sunset being the famous Southern Pacific symbol.

Near Tesnus there are two peaks called Shely Peaks which are named for the Shely family who have ranched there for many years. A few hunting seasons back, Sam Kaufman was hunting on a ranch near Shely Peaks. It was getting on toward night and all the others in the party had killed a deer except Sam. Now Sam is the most law-abiding citizen in the world who wouldn't think of breaking a law, but he tells the story of the time it looked like he would become an habitual criminal in spite of himself when he became the victim of circumstances.

When he is hunting, Sam always carries an apple in his pocket. When he gets tired or excited he eats the apple before he tries to shoot; so when he suddenly saw a big buck silhouetted against the late evening sky, that is exactly what he did. With the apple polished off, he calmly picked up his gun and shot the buck. It was then that he realized that he had broken two laws at once—first because the buck was just over the fence in another man's pasture and second because the sun had just dropped behind the hills. He scrambled up the steep mountain hoping to get his deer dressed out before

---

4. This account was taken from the records in the file of the late W. R. Mann, who was Assistant Superintendent of the Southern Pacific for many years.

dark. When he reached the buck, that Big Bender had multiplied and there lay two dead bucks—both victims of the same shot. Since one blacktail is the limit, he had now broken three laws. By the time he had finished dressing the two bucks it was pitch dark and Sam realized that he was lost. He figured the rest of the party could guide him off the mountain with flashlights if he could show them where he was, so he set a tiny fire. In no time it was spreading like gossip in a small town. Sam thought of the dollar an acre it would cost him to pay for the damaged range and he felt pretty low. There were more than one hundred thousand acres in that ranch. He had broken four laws now. The hunters in his party and a cowboy brigade spent the rest of the night fighting fire with Sam running from one to the other assuring them that he had not intended to cause any trouble at all. Sam said it was a month before he stopped looking over his shoulder for the game warden.

Haymond was named for Crede Haymond, who was a lawyer for the Southern Pacific Railroad. Though Haymond is abandoned now, it was once a busy trading post with a population of three hundred or more. Nelse Pierson owned a mercantile business, W. B. Brown was the postmaster and the Kincaids, the Combs and other ranchers traded there.

One of the Kincaid boys once loaded out a trainload of cattle and went with them to Mexico City. When his brother didn't hear from him when he thought he should, he sent the absent cattleman a telegram, asking if the cattle had sold and if he were safe. The reply was informative. "Arrived safe. Cattle sold well. Money well spent. Wire funds for a ticket home."

Marathon is a mighty high-sounding name for the little one-street cowtown that straddles the highway and railroad tracks to spread out in the Marathon Basin like a saddle blanket drying in the sun. Marathon was given its name back in 1889 when Captain Albion E. Shepherd swapped his interest in some freighters on the Great Lakes for the Iron Mountain ranch near Marathon, sight unseen. Not long after that, while working as an engineer for the Southern Pacific, he surveyed the townsite and named it Marathon, for the region is a dead ringer for that region surrounding Marathon, Greece. The Southern Pacific History states that Marathon is named for a plain in Attica.

Marathon has had a hell-for-leather past and it can live up to any tall tales told about the swagger of present-day West Texas. Though it is what Eastern visitors might call a one-horse town, some big money has changed hands there on horse races, cattle trades, land swaps and poker games. Marathon has also been the center of the rubber industry in the Big Bend and the shipping point for silver from the Boquillas Mines over one hundred miles to the south and for mercury from the quicksilver mines in Terlingua. Now the most important products shipped out of Marathon are candelilla wax and fluorspar.

Once a dude was on the observation car when the train pulled into Marathon. Roy Stillwell and Ike Gourley rode up on the crossing on their horses. The dude asked them where they got their ropes and wanted to know why they carried them on their saddles. They showed him. They caught him around the waist and pulled him off the train which left the dude tied up and stranded, for there wouldn't be another train for some time. A bunch of the cowboys showed him a good time. They gave a dance in his honor and introduced him to all the girls and he stayed around several days. When he left he had made some good friends and was glad he had been the victim of the cowboys' joke. We hope you don't have to be roped into staying around Marathon a few days to get acquainted, but if you stick around until you get to know the people, we'll bet you'll be going back.

Marathon is called the Gateway to the Big Bend National Park and when you go through, don't shut it behind you. It is a friendly town. Just because it sags in the middle, don't figure it's done for!

Alpine, thirty miles west of Marathon, has not always been called that and it came by its name as a matter of expediency.

In the early days, Kokernot Springs, then called Burgess Waterhole, was in the possession of an Irishman by the name of Murphy. This was the only water in the valley, for at that time there were no wells in the vicinity. In 1882, when the Southern Pacific was built through the Big Bend, the railroad officials found it necessary to get their water supply from Mr. Murphy. He was perfectly willing to let them have the water provided his big-heartedness be rewarded by having the station named Murphyville in his honor. The railroad people agreed, but the townspeople didn't like it one bit. They didn't think the name appropriate for a mountain village and then, too, it was too long to write when the county officials did their recording. Most of all they objected to the high-handed way Murphy had named the village.

One Sunday afternoon, Mr. Walter Garnett, Mr. C. E. Way, and Mr. Garnett's brother were talking in the back of the drugstore when the subject of the town name came up. Mr. Garnett reached over and picked up a post office directory and began thumbing through it. He happened to see the name Alpine, Alabama, and the name Alpine struck him as just the one for their town situated as it is, high in the mountains.

The next day they circulated a petition asking the government to change the name of the post office to Alpine, Texas. This name was recognized by the U.S. Post Office Department on February 3, 1888. The information furnished by the Office of the Postmaster General, Washington, D.C. states: "According to the records of the Department the post office was established under the name Murphyville in Presidio County on December 14, 1883. Mr. William H. Slaughter was the first postmaster appointed. The office was changed to Brewster County on April 13, 1887 and the name of the office was changed from Murphyville to Alpine on February 3, 1888. Mr. James Darling was postmaster at that time."

The only town in the Big Bend Country which has two main trunk lines is Alpine. The Santa Fe Railroad meets the

Southern Pacific at that place and uses the latter's tracks as far west as Paisano Pass where it cuts off to go to Presidio.

When Alpine was just getting started and did not yet have a jail, it became necessary one night to lock up a couple of questionable characters. The sheriff got permission from an official on the Southern Pacific to use a boxcar on a siding for a jail. During the night a new employee on the railroad came along and in trying to do a good job, picked up the extra car to take to San Antonio where he had a request for extra cars. Next morning the sheriff found his jail and the prisoners gone. It wasn't long until he had a message that the prisoners would be returned on the next day.

This town, straddling the Southern Pacific railroad and United States highways 90 and 67, is called the Roof Garden of Texas. It's a cowtown with a college, and the college has a million-acre campus and a cattle brand for an insignia.[5]

The Sul Ross campus, situated on College Hill, set off by the great Bar SR Bar brand outlined in whitewashed rocks set high on the mountainside behind the buildings, is an outstanding feature in Alpine. Strangers always ask how come it's called Sul Ross, and her students and those interested in her history are mighty proud to tell how Sul Ross State College was named for the famous frontier Indian fighter, Lawrence Sullivan Ross. He also served Texas as governor from 1887-91 and Texas A. & M. as president from 1891-98, the date of his death. Sul Ross State College has made educational history on the last frontier of Texas and does honor to the famous frontiersman for whom it is named.

Sul Ross enrolled its first class in the summer of 1920 and was authorized to offer work for a bachelor's degree in 1924.

---

5. When the Big Benders were working hard to get Big Bend National Park established, they often referred to the proposed park as a million-acre campus for Sul Ross. Students of geology, biology and botany use the Park as a great outdoor laboratory.

By 1935, a full program for both bachelor's and master's degrees was offered.

Names of pioneer cattlemen are associated with the development of Sul Ross. The late J. D. Jackson was called the father of the college because of the work he did in getting it established in Alpine. He donated the land on which Jackson Field, the home of the Lobos, is built.

J. D. Jackson gave much of his time, money, and energy to the Texas Cattleman's Association and helped build it into one of the leading institutions of the West. It was at an annual meeting of the Cattleman's Association held in Houston, Texas, March 21, 1916, that the Honorable Thomas Ball, on behalf of the Houston Chamber of Commerce, presented J. D. Jackson with a badge of pure gold, set with diamonds. In presenting the badge, Mr. Ball said, "Its pure gold is typical of everlasting friendship; the diamonds which sparkle upon the virgin gold will serve as a brilliant reminder of the bond created between the representatives of one of the greatest industries in Texas and the future great city of the Southwest. When you wear it—and may you wear it through a long and happy life—let your heart turn with pleasant recollections to the days when the Fortieth Annual Meeting of the Cattleman's Association was held in the City of Houston."

J. D. Jackson was a great and generous man, a loyal friend, and a builder of fine things. His memory will live in the history of the Big Bend Country and in the hearts of all Sul Ross alumni.

Dr. Benjamin F. Berkeley shares the stage with J. D. Jackson in the role they played together to bring about the establishment of Sul Ross. They both spent a great deal of time in Austin lobbying for the project. Dr. Berkeley spent the entire time of the legislative session in 1917 in Austin, telling representatives and senators how essential it was to establish a college in his part of the state. They got their college.

Hancock Hall for Men was named in honor of W. B. Hancock, prominent rancher and citizen, who donated one hundred acres of land for the Sul Ross Campus. Kokernot

Park and Lodge are built on land donated to Sul Ross by H. L. Kokernot.

Sul Ross put some of her classes on wheels, and students make trips to all points in the United States and Mexico, building better relations between her students and those of other colleges. The students earn credits in various fields by writing about their experiences and reporting on their research.

Sul Ross State College has been a great influence in building better relations between Mexico and Texas, and is training leaders and teachers who will use their training to raise the standards of living in both population groups.

Most visitors to the Big Bend take a short side trip to Old Fort Davis, about twenty-five miles northwest of Alpine on Highway 118. Fort Davis, established on October 7, 1854, was named for Jefferson Davis, then Secretary of War. The picturesque abandoned fort lies in the heart of the Davis Mountain country, a truly spectacular region with a history and personality all its own, with such outstanding attractions as beautiful Indian Lodge, noted for its fine tourist accomodations; the McDonald Observatory on Mt. Locke; the scenic loop drive around Mt. Livermore; and the Prude Guest Ranch, known for its fine ranch food and genuine western hospitality.

Bloys Camp Meeting, held in Skillman's Grove in the Davis Mountains, is an institution known all over the nation. For one week in August, since its establishment back in 1890, great religious leaders have delivered unforgettable sermons in an unforgettable setting. Bloys Camp Meeting was named in honor of the late Rev. W. B. Bloys, one of the founders, and Skillman's Grove was named for Henry Skillman, a frontiersman who stood off an Apache attack on the mail wagon from the shelter of live oaks in the grove.

After the scenic drive through the Davis Mountain country, one of the oldest vacation spots in the Trans-Pecos region, visitors usually return to Alpine to continue their tour of the Big Bend Country.

Halfway between Alpine and Marfa is Paisano, the summit of the Sunset Route and the home of the Paisano Baptist Encampment. Paisano is a Spanish word meaning countryman.

Marfa, about twenty-five miles west of Alpine, was named by the wife of the chief engineer of the railroad for the heroine of a Russian novel she was reading at the time that a name was to be given to the new watering place on the line. J. M. Dean, an attorney of El Paso, bought the land around the railroad station of Marfa. Mr. Dean was a man who took what he wanted when he wanted it, so when he decided that he wanted a county seat on his section of land he just went to Fort Davis, took the Presidio County records and brought them to Marfa. About this time an election was held, "legal and everything," to move the county seat from Fort Davis to Marfa. The election resulted in a vote of 390 to 302, so Mr. Dean got his county seat. Some people thought he had used highhanded, selfish, and ruthless methods, so the people of Fort Davis and Alpine just had their parts of Presidio County cut off, thus creating Jeff Davis and Brewster counties.[6]

Marfa is a progressive town, and the home of the Highland Hereford Association. It is also the home of a lot of mighty friendly people who like to say "Howdy" to strangers. To make sure they get that chance, Marfa installed a traffic light —at present the only one in the Big Bend Country.

Ryan is a stock shipping station where often whole trains of livestock are loaded. Ryan was named for Mr. Black Ryan who was Land Commissioner for the Southern Pacific lines about 1882.

Valentine was named for President Valentine of the Wells–Fargo Company. The store at Valentine was robbed by Black Jack Ketchum back in the middle 1890's. Before he left the store he took most of the stock of candy, the surest proof that

6. Mrs. O. L. Shipman, *Taming the Big Bend,* Marfa, Texas, 1926, pp. 55-56.

the robber was Black Jack, because his love of candy was known to all who knew him well.

Two other versions of how come Valentine is called that are given by old-timers. One is that the first train sent through that station stopped there on St. Valentine's Day and the other is that the town was named for Longfellow's poem of that name.

Chapter 7

SOUTHWEST BIG BEND AND DOWN THE RIO GRANDE

D*ROPPING AWAY* from the tracks at Valentine toward the Rio Grande, you cross the region where much of the activity in the early development of the region took place. The history of the Indian and Spanish periods is centered in and around this section.

For this account of recent and completely modern development we are indebted to Barry Scobee of Fort Davis: "The rugged and lofty Viejo Mountains, 15 air miles southwest of Valentine and 20 miles from the Rio Grande, have been selected as the site for a radar defense station and is expected to be in full operation about January of 1957.

"Since the beginning of Army activities in extreme West Texas in the days of warring Apaches a hundred years ago this immediate area has heard the gallop of cavalry horses, and in later years the chugging of army motors.

"In the Indian days, old War Department records reveal, when an officer or a sergeant led a detachment of cavalry or mounted infantry after raiding redskins, on their return to the post they were required to draw sketches of their routes. They show pursuits to the vicinity of the Viejo Mountain range and to nearby Capote Mountain on the ranch of the late L. C. Brite and on southward to the Rio Grande. Peaks in the Viejos—a Spanish word meaning old or antiquated—attain a height of more than 6,000 feet. Viejo Peak itself is shown as 6,467 feet in elevation.

"During World War I the government constructed three forts or camps in this region bordering Mexico. One was at Castalon that is now near Big Bend National Park. Another was not far from Viejo near the Rio Grande. The third was 20 miles north of the river, which was called Camp Holland, named for the one-time owner of the land. It is owned now by Espy Miller and is about six miles west of the site of the planned Valentine Air Force Station."[1]

Directly south of Valentine one can see Capote Mountain where the headquarters of the L. C. Brite ranch are located. *Capote* is the Spanish word for cape, and from a distance the mountain does look like a spread-out cape. Along the top are some ripples which look a little like the teeth of a saw, so some people refer to it as Sawtooth Mountain.

Back in 1870, William Russell established a sheep ranch at the foot of Capote. The Indians had never molested the settlements along this portion of the Rio Grande before, because they lay some distance from their trails, but the Apaches did raid the sheep ranch at Capote and only one of the herders escaped.

About 1885, L. C. Brite drove his first herd of cattle to the range near Capote. He reported that long dusty lines of cattle, sometimes representing five or six different brands, could be seen winding their way into the valley. The beauty and charm around Capote impressed him even then, but to most of the cowboys it was just the end of the trail where they could rest after many days in the saddle and nights of riding out stampedes and standing night guard. The ranch developed at Capote is considered one of the outstanding ranches in the Big Bend Country, and it is still owned by Mrs. L. C. Brite.

One of the worst raids on the Texas border was one carried out against the Brite ranch on Christmas Day, 1917. The story of the Brites of Capote is so unusual and interesting that it was used as the subject of a book by that name and was written by Noel L. Keith. From 1885 until the time of this writing, the Brites of Capote have figured prominently

---

1. Barry Scobee, "Valentine Radar Plan Offers Ranchmen Roads and Power," San Angelo *Standard-Times,* Oct. 16, 1955.

in all civic and religious development in the town of Marfa and the county of Presidio and the state of Texas.

West of Capote and a few miles up the Rio Grande is situated the adobe village of Porvenir. Little more than a stone's throw above this village, the Rio Grande swings to the south to begin its big bend which gives the region its name. *Porvenir* is the Spanish word for future—a misnomer if there was ever one, for Porvenir seems to have little future. But anything can happen in the Big Bend Country and usually does, so Porvenir could possibly become the center of a great mineral development.

Just below Porvenir on the Rio Grande is the village of Pilares which gets its name from the Spanish word meaning waterhole. Pilares was established about 1775 as a military and penal colony, and the convicts and soldiers were required to work on the farms there. From all signs, the smelting of silver ore was carried on extensively. The presidio there was abandoned about 1873.[2]

Pilares has always been a hot spot for crime and during the bandit raids on the border, it seemed that all the trails to trouble led to Pilares. It was to investigate the situation there that Rangers Trollinger and Cummings, and Mounted Inspector Craighead, with Inspector Joe Sitters and Ranger Hulen, left Valentine on the morning of May 21, 1915, for a scout on the river. At Pilares some of Villa's soldiers reported to the scouts that a band of Mexican bandits was hiding in the mountains on this side of the river with a big bunch of smuggled horses and mules. The next morning the officers picked up their trail and about dusk came upon a part of the horses guarded by three men. A running fight took place but the bandits escaped. The next day they again took up the trail and the battle was reported by the survivors:

"The next morning, May 24, we went on up into the

2. Carl Graham Raht, *Romance of the Davis Mountains,* p. 120.

mountains. Mr. Sitters being in command, divided our party, sending we three, Craighead, Trollinger and Cummings, up a canyon, while he and Ranger Hulen climbed a peak to get a view of the surrounding country. We were to try to get the horses, which were up against a bluff, while he kept a lookout for the Mexicans.

"As soon as we were in the canyon the Mexicans began firing on us from all sides. They had allowed us to pass them where they were hiding until we were entirely surrounded. As soon as the shooting began we dismounted, took our guns and cartridges, and sought shelter behind the boulders and rocks.

"Our party tried five different times to get to where Sitters and Hulen were, but it was impossible, and Sitters waved and called to us to go back. We could see them but were unable to see the Mexicans. After four hours of slowly working our way back over the mountains under heavy fire we gained a position back of where Sitters and Hulen had been last seen, but they had changed their position.

"We decided to try to get out, as we were badly outnumbered and were famished for water. When we had finally worked our way out of range of the Mexicans' guns the firing ceased and we knew Sitters and Hulen were either dead or had made their escape.

"We walked about five miles to a water hole, suffering terribly from thirst. There we found four head of loose stock, which we drove to where we had left our pack outfit that morning. We roped them with pack ropes and put our pack saddles on them. They were so poor we could not ride much but walked and rode together until we reached the McGee ranch which was about five miles farther on.

"We reached there about dusk and sent a Mexican with a note asking for help to the John Pool ranch, six miles away over the mountains. From this ranch the news was scattered over the surrounding country and a posse of men was organized at Marfa, forty miles away, and came to the Pool ranch in automobiles. They mounted there and came to the McGee ranch, reaching there about sun-up. A small party also came from Valentine.

"We reached the mountain pass where the fight occurred about 3 o'clock in the afternoon of May 25 and there found the mutilated bodies of Sitters and Hulen lying about thirty yards apart.

"Sitters had made a brave fight. It being evident from the shells surrounding his body that he had fired about sixty shots. Hulen was wounded early in the fight and was only to fire one shot. We tied their bodies on a pack mule and took them to the McGee ranch where we buried them side by side in the same grave. It was impossible to bring them any nearer home.

"The bandits probably went back over the river, as we found no trace of them. They took our horses and saddles and rifled the pockets of the two men they killed. They killed Sitters' horse and left him with the saddle on. There were between thirty and thirty-five men in the Mexican band."[3]

The deaths of Texas Ranger Hulen and Customs Inspector Joe Sitters were a great loss to the Big Bend Country, for the men had served the region well. It was said of Joe Sitters that "he could read a trail like a signboard, trail a cottontail rabbit across a rocky hill or track a bobcat through a nopal (prickly pear) and chaparral thicket." Luke Dowe of Del Rio said, "Joe wasn't what you'd call a rough man. He had a kindly pair of eyes, a kindly voice. Those eyes never let him miss a thing. He was cool, unexcitable, but he could be as stern as the barrel of a .45-Colt with the hammer cocked back."

About twenty-five miles down the Rio Grande from Pilares is the village of Candelaria, which, according to the old Mexicans, was named for a woman who had unusual powers. Another version of the story is that *candelaria* is a Spanish word for the candles used in religious ceremonies. At the village

3. San Antonio *Express,* May 31, 1915.

of Candelaria the formation of the rocks looks very much like candles. They are tall sandstone pinnacles eroded by the water to resemble a candelabrum.

In 1868, William Russell established a farm at Candelaria to raise grain to supply Fort Davis and Fort Stockton. There are farms in that area yet.

Down the river from Candelaria is the little settlement of Ruidosa, which is the Spanish word for noisy or windy, and it came by its name because the wind blows there most of the year and is especially noisy during the spring. There are hot springs near Ruidosa where people go to take baths which are said to cure everything except laziness.

Pinto Canyon runs from Ruidosa into the Chinati Mountains. Pinto Canyon means painted canyon and gets its name from the brilliant colors of its walls.

In the foothills of the Chinati Mountains is the village of the same name. Both mountain and village were so-named because many blackbirds were seen there and *chinati* is the Spanish word for blackbirds. Another version of how Chinati came by its name is that it was the name of an Indian chief. Early histories mention Chief Chinati. He was supposed to be prominent around 1840 to 1850.

On Highway 67 between Marfa and Presidio is the town of Shafter which at the time of this writing is a ghost town, but rumors float along the highway and along the river that the ghost is coming to life. Shafter, where millions of dollars worth of silver were mined in the tunnels under the Chinati, now looks as if an atomic bomb had done its worst, but the heart of the Chinati is rich in minerals and in legend and there are prospectors for both.

Once a Mexican went to Tom Skaggs at Lajitas and asked if he would accompany him on an expedition of investigation. Mr. Skaggs never knew whether he missed finding a cache of gold and a dead Indian, or having his own throat slit, for he did not volunteer to go. Over on the creek near Shafter there was a cave in which an Indian had been left to guard some gold that a band of Indians had stolen from a stagecoach, and the cave had been closed with rocks, leaving the Indian with an old rifle locked within. Some soldiers were pressing the Indians closely which was the reason they hid the gold in the cave, but it seems that the soldiers killed some of the band and chased the others so far into Mexico that they never returned for the gold or to extricate the Indian guard left in the cave. True to his duty he died there, waiting with an ancient rifle across his knees. There is hardly a cave in the Chinati without its legend of buried treasure.

Shafter was named for General W. R. Shafter, who was once stationed at Fort Davis. The silver ore was discovered by John W. Spencer in 1883, according to some reports, but an Indian scout took Lieutenant Bullis to the mine much earlier than that and Bullis is said to have been the first white man to enter the mine. However the samples which Spencer took to General Shafter were assayed and as a result of the reports the Shafter Mining Company was organized in 1885. It was officially closed on January 1, 1942. W. S. Noyes, first superintendent of the Shafter mines, told W. D. Burcham that he started there in 1882, so apparently there was some reorganization of the mine in 1885. General Bullis was one of the first members of the company, along with General Shafter and John W. Spencer.

It would be interesting to know how those who named the place decided to call the town Shafter instead of Spencer, Bullis or Chinati. In time we believe this story will come to light. "*¿Quién sabe?*"

Shafter and the surrounding area made up the empire ranch of the Big Bend's first cattleman, Don Milton Faver. His three main ranches were Cibolo (buffalo), Cienega (marsh) and Morita (mulberry). Much has been written about Milton Faver's herds being unbranded. There were wild Mexican longhorns and Milton Faver's cowboys had no horses. They rode burros. When the Texas ranchmen came into the region with good horses, some of them helped Don Milton brand his cattle and others just helped themselves to his cattle. Milton Faver's brand was changed into a dozen strange brands.[4]

Don Milton arrived in the Big Bend in a hack with all the modern appointments, attended by a colony of servants. He was a gentleman who treated his guests with hospitality. Some thought that the evident marks of good breeding seemed incongruous in his frontier surroundings. He married a Mexican woman of quality and they had one son, Juan, who was educated in the best schools. Some of Don Milton's grandchildren and great-grandchildren still live in the Big Bend Country.

On the Chihuahua Trail not far from Shafter was a place called La Posta, Spanish for "the post." It was a stopping place for travelers on the stage which carried the mail to Presidio.

It was while Mr. and Mrs. R. E. L. Tyler were living at The Post and getting rich from the good meals that Mrs. Tyler cooked for the travelers, that their neighbors, the James Walkers, raised a big bunch of turkeys. Jim hated those turkeys because his wife made him herd them out in the pasture where the grasshoppers were swarming. He figured that was not a fitting occupation for a man, so one day while he was out with the flock, he drove them fourteen miles over the mountain to The Post and offered them to the Tylers. After some horse-trading, he sold them for twenty cents a head—the whole two hundred of them—and for months the Tylers served turkey to the travelers, making an enormous profit.[5]

It wasn't long until Mr. and Mrs. Tyler had saved enough money to buy a ranch. They drove over to see Mrs. Bishop, Mrs. Tyler's mother, and asked her if she would sell her ranch. For $600 on the barrelhead, she would. Mrs. Tyler

---

4. Personal interviews with Mrs. John Humphris and Mr. T. C. Mitchell.

5. Mr. Tyler told this story to Mrs. Oren Bunton and she passed it on to us with Mr. Tyler's permission.

reached down in her stocking, came up with a big roll and peeled off the $600. Then she told Mr. Tyler to go to Marfa and fix up the papers to prove their ownership. After a little investigation, Mr. Tyler found that Mrs. Bishop didn't even own the land. She had missed her payments and the land had reverted to the state. But Mr. Tyler was not going to be done out of the ranch; so he filed on the land, paid the state $1.00 an acre and Mrs. Bishop kept her $600.[6]

When Bill Bunton bought The Post and the range land from Bill McGee, he changed the name to La Posta. The Buntons were folks who liked Mexican names. Today Mrs. Oren Bunton of Marfa owns La Posta.

About twenty-one miles south of Shafter on Highway 67 is the town of Presidio, which was old historically even before the first American settled there in 1843. It has been known by many names. Cabeza de Vaca stopped there on his wanderings through Texas and erected a cross on the mountain side, calling the place Las Cruces. In 1681 the settlement became known as La Junta, meaning The Junction, because the Rio Conchos flows into the Rio Grande at a point just above the village. A hundred years later, a Jumano Indian, Juan Sabeata by name, told Governor Cruzate at Paso del Norte (now El Paso) about a flaming cross on the mountain, so in 1683 La Junta became known as La Navidad in Las Cruces. About 1760 the settlement became a penal colony and a military garrison of sixty men. Then came the military organization known as the Flying Squadron, and the settlement took on more dignity as Presidio del Norte. It retained this title until the War of 1847 between the United States and Mexico, at which time the settlement was divided by the International Boundary, the Rio Grande. The Mexican settlement on the opposite bank of the river became known as Ojinaga, while early maps began to carry the name Rancho Spencer where today lies Presidio proper.

Presidio today is a quiet border town where descendants

6. *Ibid.*

of the founding fathers carry on the work and traditions of those pioneers. But Presidio has not always been quiet! When the United States troops were stationed on the Texas border at Presidio and Pancho Villa operated in and around Ojinaga in Mexico, there was plenty of excitement and rumors created much tension. In the summer of 1957, Mrs. I. L. Kleinman of San Antonio, formerly of Presidio, Texas, told this story:

"My husband I. L. Kleinman operated a general merchandise store at Presidio for many years. The living quarters of the family, the store proper, and the warehouses adjoined one another, the whole being enclosed by a high wall made of adobe bricks, topped with broken pieces of glass embedded in the adobe.

"About 1914 when Pancho Villa was operating in the Mexican country across the river from the Big Bend District, United States troops were stationed at Presidio. The army camp was about three-quarters of a mile from our store. Because Mr. Kleinman had a considerable stock of sporting fire arms and ammunition, a sentinel was placed around the store at night. I had not been informed of this action. One evening, after a particularly trying day, filled with rumors that Villa was going to cross the river and sack Presidio, I looked out my bed room window, and to my horror saw a big man with a rifle on his shoulder pass by. I immediately assumed that he was a Villaista and that Presidio was about to be sacked.

"I tried to whisper what I had seen to Mr. Kleinman, but as he was partially deaf, and I was afraid to talk loud, it was some time before he understood what I had seen. During the interval of suspense my husband would stand in front of the window, and to complicate matters I was trying to get him to move as well as tell him about the man I had seen. When he finally understood what I was trying to convey to him, he became almost as excited as I was. He rushed to the building occupied by the clerks, woke them up and had them arm themselves to be ready to ward off the attack. Mr. Kleinman then investigated the outside of the establishment, and you can't realize how happy I was when the Villaista turned out to be a United States cavalryman, walking his post."

All over the country there are retired Army personnel who will remember, with nostalgia, days spent on tours of duty at Presidio, Texas. Col. H. M. Henderson, retired, who now lives in San Antonio, told us two stories about Army life in the Big Bend.

THE OLDEST LIEUTENANT IN THE WORLD

In 1916 there was stationed at Sierra Blanca, Texas, a first lieutenant of cavalry, who claimed not only to be the oldest lieutenant in the United States Army, but the oldest lieutenant in the world.

He was a distinguished-looking officer. He had an abundant suit of hair and it was silver white, as were his long full beard and mustachios.

A company of National Guard Infantry, commanded by a young captain, was ordered to Sierra Blanca for duty. The captain wanted very much to secure a commission in the regular army, which he later did. As the train pulled up to the station platform in Sierra Blanca the captain, who was observing everything with a keen eye, noted that a very distinguished-looking officer, who could be no less than a brigadier general, was meeting the train. The captain rushed up to the officer, gave him a snappy and proper salute. When he looked at the insignia of his shirt collar the captain could hardly believe his eyes, for pinned on the collar were the silver bars of a first lieutenant.

In June of 1916, the old lieutenant was promoted to captain and transferred to Presidio. One night he was officer of the day at this post. Around two o'clock in the morning he was trying to locate a cossack post which was posted in an arroyo bed, west of camp. This post was hard to find at night as the ground was covered with brush and there were no definite landmarks. He hunted and hunted and finally almost ran into the sentry. He said to the sentry, "Why in the hell didn't you challenge me? I have been walking around in this area for the past thirty minutes looking for you." The sentry replied, "Sir, I have been challenging burros all night and I thought you were another burro."

This same captain of the silvery white hair and beard owned a horse named Do Dos Do. At that time officers of cavalry had to take an annual test ride, known as the Russian Ride. It consisted of a ride of several miles over a number of obstacles. Do Dos Do had the reputation of knocking down every jump he attempted to take, so when the annual ride came up at Presidio, Do Dos Do led off in the course. He would knock down all the jumps and the other officers could clear the obstacles with ease.

Between Presidio and the junction of Alamito Creek and the Rio Grande is the famous Presidio County landmark known as Old Fortin or Fort Leaton, established in 1848 by Ben Leaton. Its construction was said to have been completed by John Burgess. Fort Leaton was the site of one of the seven presidios established in the vicinity of La Junta or the junction of the Rio Grande and the Rio Conchos.

Ben Leaton had much influence on the development of the area around Presidio and there are two schools of thought as to whether that influence was good or bad. Perhaps it was a little bit of both. Some thought his trade and treaties with the Indians caused the United States much trouble, but others say that Ben Leaton has never been given credit for what he did in the early days. Certainly many early travelers and settlers might have died of thirst and starvation had he not been there to help them out.

Just below Fort Leaton and about six miles below Presidio, Alamito Creek runs into the Rio Grande. The Creek gets its name from the Spanish word meaning poplar or cottonwood. The Alamito is long indeed, running from the Davis Mountains through Marfa and on to the Rio Grande. John Davis established a settlement in 1870 about thirty miles below Marfa on this creek and the settlement was called Alamito.

Mrs. Esther Russell Devine, granddaughter of William Russell, one of the very first settlers in the Presidio area, told us this story of her family history—history which was made at two well-known ranches along the Alamito Creek.

"The Alamo Ranch got its name from a big lone *alamo* (cottonwood) tree and the Alamito Creek which runs through it with springs just below the house. This ranch, located about sixty miles south of Marfa, Texas, was homesteaded in 1874 by Victoriano Hernandez. He owned it and lived there until his death by accidental drowning in a water hole at the Alamo Springs in the year 1903.

"He homesteaded and 'patented' the land on which the house and garden are situated. There are only ruins left of the buildings, and the fruit trees are all dead, but in the past there were pears, figs, peaches and pomegranates.

"The old ranch house consisted of eight large rooms with a patio on the east side, built of adobe brick: all doors and windows were brought from Mexico, and very crudely made, wooden pegs were used mostly, but a few square handmade nails were found in some of the doors and frames.

"The Chapel was built about 1889 after the death of Oscar Duke, Victoriano's grandson. This building was made of the same materials. Victoriano Hernandez settled at the Alamo Ranch and there reared his family of five sons and three daughters. He and his wife, Nicomedes, were a very hard-working couple and soon had a thriving ranch with the help of his sons, and few ranch hands. One of the ranch hands was an ex-slave called Clemente.

"The Mescalero Apaches had not been removed to their reservation in New Mexico and they roamed the hills at will, but they were friendly with the family and never made any trouble for them. As Hernandez and his sons prospered, rumors were circulated that he was a miser and had his money buried about the ranch and other ridiculous tales were spread.

"The ranch house, sitting by the main road was open to guests at all times. The ranch was a stopping place for wagon trains travelling between San Antonio and Presidio. One day a lone man rode up to the house and was invited to dismount and rest. He accepted the invitation but soon left, saying that he had a long distance to travel. Mrs. Hernandez was not present when he left and when she saw him riding away she was disturbed because he did not stay for the noon meal. Hurriedly she packed some food and sent her grandson, Oscar, to call the man and give him the lunch. This he did.

"That same evening the family was sitting in the east patio resting after the evening meal, as was their custom. Suddenly the Negro, Clemente, rushed in and called to them to go in the house, quickly, as the ranch was being attacked by robbers. Victoriano did not have time to close the front door, which faced the west so he tried to hold it and was wounded in the left arm. Gilberto Hernandez, one of the sons, was inside and returned the fire. Believing there were other men inside, the robbers retreated. During the assault the robbers had been shooting through the window where Mrs. Hernandez and the children had taken refuge. Oscar Duke, trying to cross the room, was mortally wounded and died almost instantly. (The man to whom he had taken the lunch was a member of the robber band.)

"Victoriano Hernandez was a very religious man. After the death of Oscar Duke, he built a small Chapel over the grave. From Ojinaga, Chihuahua, Mexico, he brought a Statue of Christ on the Cross. Walking and carrying the four foot Statue on his back, he left Ojinaga at sundown and arrived at the Alamo Ranch the next morning, a distance of thirty miles over mountainous country.

"However, all was not sorrow and tragedy at the Alamo Ranch. There were many happy weddings, baptisms and events taking place in the little Chapel which was built in memory of the ten-year old Oscar. The old Alamo Ranch is very scenic, has excellent all-year climate. The water from the springs is sweet and cool coming out of the limestone. Some day it may again be a happy thriving ranch; at least such are the hopes and prayers of the present owner, Mrs. Lucia H. Russell, granddaughter of Victoriano Hernandez. Mrs. Russell, and some of the other 'old timers' still remember the joys and laughter of the pioneers who homesteaded the Alamo and other ranches. They also remember the friendly Indians and the many wagon trains going through and all stopping over night.

"Mrs. Lucia Hernandez Russell is my mother. Her father and grandfather lived at Alamo Ranch, but when she married William Russell they bought Casa Piedra Ranch, about 42 miles south of Marfa and 22 miles north of Presidio. There they raised nine children and lost one. Those living are Anita, Robert, Esther (me) Tomasa, Willie, Joe, Laura, Elva, and Jean. None live at the ranch with Mrs. Russell. Casa Piedra derived its name from the fact that the first house there was built of rock but now everything in that part of the country is built of adobe."

Down the Rio Grande about sixteen miles below Presidio is the little settlement called Polvo (Spanish for dust) by the Mexicans and Redford by the Anglo-Americans. The sandstone is of a reddish color in this area and it serves as a crossing for the people, so the village takes its name from a combination of the two—and is called Redford. When Dr. Robert T. Hill explored the Rio Grande in 1899, he called the place Polvo and the early maps are marked with that name.

Col. H. M. Henderson told us this story of army life and its hazards in the Big Bend Country around Polvo.

THE DUSTY INSPECTION

In late 1916 a company of infantry, along with several other companies and troops of cavalry, was stationed at Presidio,

Texas. The company in question was split up, one platoon being located at Polvo, about twenty-two miles as the soldiers marched down the Rio Grande, and the other platoon at Indio, twenty-two miles up the river. The company headquarters were at Presidio.

One day a rather elderly lieutenant colonel of the Inspector General's Department appeared to conduct the annual inspection of troops. The young captain of the split-up company was strong and active, and rode a tough Wyoming horse loaned him by a medical officer. The horse was young and in fine shape. He could take a fast trot and keep it for hours. The company commander visited at least one of the platoons each week, the distance being covered in a little less than two hours. The only way one could get to Polvo was by walking or riding a horse or in an escort wagon, the road was too rough for an automobile.

The company commander decided that the trip to Polvo with the lieutenant colonel would be a fine chance to give him a good workout and see whether he could ride or not. The lieutenant colonel was told of the limited ways of getting to Polvo, and the company commander also said that he would make arrangements with the cavalry for a mount for him. The inspector said, "You say there are only two ways of getting to Polvo, on a horse or in a wagon?" "Yes, sir, that is correct," replied the company commander. "In that case then you order the platoon at Polvo to march to Presidio, and I will inspect them here."

The little infantry platoon marched from Polvo to Presidio, were inspected, and marched back to their station the next day.

"I doubt if the inspector put that in his book," laughed Colonel Henderson.

Since Polvo is a long and dusty march from Presidio, we can be sure that for that platoon of soldiers, Polvo (dust) has a very special meaning.

Down the river from Redford (Polvo) runs a canyon known as Contrabando which got its name because the *contrabandistas* traveled through this canyon and over a mountain by the same name on their way to and from their market places with their contraband goods. In the early 1900's the tariff laws were held to be unjust by a large part of the inhabitants of the region around Presidio and by all those traveling the Contrabando Trail. These *contrabandistas* smuggled going and coming, and dealt in all kinds of trade without paying duty to the governments of Mexico or Texas. Though livestock dealing was the biggest trade of the *contrabandistas,* some dealt in liquor, smuggled over in pig bladders and goatskins which were easy to fasten to pack mules and in case of accidents were not easily broken. After delivery to retailers it was put in bottles and jugs for sale to customers.

One class of *contrabandistas* who neatly evaded the duties were those who engaged in smuggling merchandise to Mexico. They were for the most part natives of Mexico and traveled a hundred miles through Texas to railroad towns where they received shipments of materials, packed it on mules or burros and leisurely but secretively transported it to the river, smuggled it across and carried it miles to the larger towns in Mexico. This trade became so important and disturbing to the government of Mexico that the *fiscales* or river guards were offered, in addition to their salaries, one-half of all the contraband captured by them. This almost stopped the business for awhile, but those who traveled the Contrabando Trail soon learned to evade the *fiscales* and the trail was not abandoned for many years.

Lajitas lies just outside the western extremity of the Big Bend National Park. It gets its name from the Spanish word meaning flat rocks or flagstones. Lajitas was once a port of entry and was occupied by American troops. In its heyday of prosperous trade, Lajitas was about the sorest spot on the border. Pancho Villa dominated a large part of the state of Chihuahua, using it as an outlet and inlet for the greatest flow of stock stealing and munition running that ever existed anywhere. When peace came to the border country, it smothered the life out of Lajitas which eventually became a ghost town. Then, even in the glaring sunshine, you felt the presence of ghosts and would find yourself turning quickly to see if someone was watching you, and likely as not someone was, for Mexican sentinels sat folded into stumplike figures along the high ridges of both sides of the river. No one ever approached Lajitas unseen or unannounced.

Then came the discovery of uranium and Lajitas came to life like the Resurrection Plant. The store at Lajitas became the busiest place in the Big Bend. Abandoned adobe houses are now renting for good prices to serve as offices, dining rooms and living quarters for the uranium mining interests. And the government price support program on quicksilver caused a flurry in the quicksilver industry, and the old abandoned mines are reopening and new prospecting is going on. The region around Lajitas and Lajitas itself is owned by Rex Ivey. Tourists in the Big Bend National Park seldom miss a trip to Lajitas because it is one of the most interesting places along the river and the Iveys are mighty nice folks to know.

At present there are only two routes out of and into the Big Bend National Park, but when the proposed highway is built, linking the western edge of the park with Presidio, the tourists will have an opportunity to see some of the most beautiful scenery in the Big Bend Country. They will come in contact with place names seldom mentioned out of the region itself, and they will become familiar with the earliest history of the Big Bend. This proposed highway will be known as the Treasure Trail because over it were carried the treasures of the Spanish explorers and those who came after them, and along this trail were buried many of the treasures which never reached their destinations. It is appropriately named, for it is a Treasure Trail in lore and in scenic beauty.

From Presidio to Redford the road is paved, but from Redford to the western entrance of the park, Treasure Trail is full of hazards in its present condition. It was approximately this route that the camel caravan traveled in its search for a good location for the sub-station for the army back in 1860. Santana Mesa, named for an Indian Chief, is about seven hundred feet above the Rio Grande, and on the shoulder of the slope there is a spot from which to view the Rio Grande Valley and the canyon walls on the Mexican side.

Moving on toward Lajitas, the road skirts Colorado Canyon (named for its red coloring), crosses the Fowlkes Brothers Ranch, circles a range of hills, then leads across a couple of draws before it spans Fresno Creek, named for the Fresno trees, near the Decie fishing lodge. Then it circles Contrabando waterhole and follows around Contrabando Mountain and Lajitas Mesa. The trail lies a little more than a mile north of Lajitas and runs along the side of the mountain where the quicksilver mines are. From Lajitas it is only a few miles east to the junction with Highway 118, which is the western entrance of the Big Bend National Park. The circle is complete.

On November 4th and 5th in 1961, the Big Bend National Park Development Committee invited about 3000 guests to the official opening of the scenic river road. This Ranch-to-Market road No. 170 crosses and recrosses the old trail over which the Spanish explorers carried their treasures and subsequently smugglers moved their clandestine cargoes on pack-laden burros. This route was first called Treasure Trail, as was noted on page 117, but at the official opening of the road the name was changed.

To interest the young people in the opening of the new road, the schools held a contest to choose a name. Juan Nieto, a school boy from Presidio and Grace Humphreys of Marfa won the contest. So it was that the new Highway linking Presidio, Texas and Ojinaga, Mexico to the western entrance of the Big Bend National Park became known as Camino del Rio.

EPILOGUE

PERHAPS BY NOW it will be easy to understand why some of the place names are drab and uninteresting, while others are mysterious, thought-provoking or appropriately descriptive. The Mexicans living along the Rio Grande, the old-timers and early cattlemen know the region well, but they are silent people and have recorded little of their information. But when they are approached with a direct question, they give a direct answer and when that answer is written down, another bit of history has been preserved.

Those who went to explore and left a record of what they saw have voiced opinions which lead readers to believe that they explored different regions. For example, during the bandit raids along the Rio Grande and at Glenn Springs, James Hooper was in the Big Bend Country writing a series of articles for *Collier's* magazine. A newsreel cameraman was sent there to record the situation on film and he said to Hooper, "Everyone in that Big Bend Country is of a kind I never saw before." And in describing the country from Marathon to the Rio Grande he said, "The country isn't bad. It's just worse. Worse the moment you set foot from the train, and then, after that, just worser and worser." Those remarks were made in the spring of 1916. But in February of 1956, Ludwig Bemelmans, writer and artist, traveling the selfsame route says of the same region in his article in *McCall's,* "In a lifetime spent in traveling, here I came upon the greatest wonder. The mantle of God touches you; it is what Beethoven reached for in music; it is panorama without beginning or end."[1] It's no wonder then that some believe the Big Bend to be a state of mind, for geologists, historians, artists, speculators, cowboys and bandits looked at the Big Bend at different seasons, under different conditions, in different moods and for different reasons and to each it gave back a story to suit the point of view. And for that reason the Big Bend has been variously described as "our last frontier," "the Playground of the Gods," "the greatest geological textbook in the world," "the end of nowhere," "cow heaven," "a haven for those who want to disappear," "a desert wasteland," "a hard, cruel, brigand-infested region," "a *zona libre* (free zone)." Whatever else the Big Bend is, it is a chameleon region—a magnet to the adventuresome spirit.

All over the Big Bend Country there are mountain peaks, draws, spectacularly beautiful and interesting places with no names to identify them. But in time all the places will be named, and when they are we hope much thought and study will be given to the naming so that there will be just reasons for *How Come It's Called That*.

---

1. Ludwig Bemelmans, *op. cit.*, p. 24.

INDEX

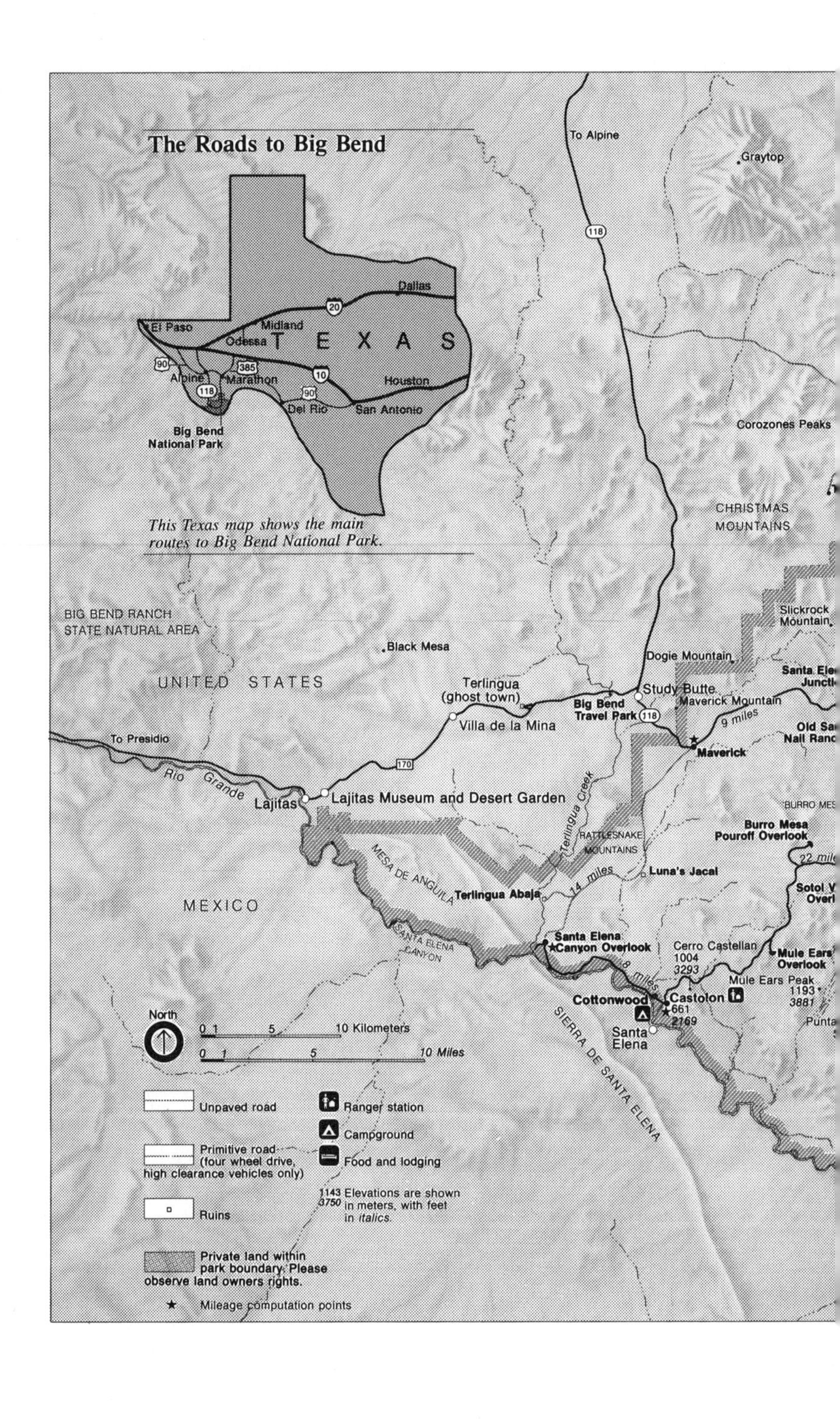
The Roads to Big Bend
Dallas
20
El Paso
Midland
Odessa
T E X A S
90
385
10
Alpine
Marathon
Houston
118
90
Del Rio
San Antonio
Big Bend
National Park
This Texas map shows the main routes to Big Bend National Park.
To Alpine
Graytop
118
Corozones Peaks
CHRISTMAS
MOUNTAINS
Slickrock
Mountain
BIG BEND RANCH
STATE NATURAL AREA
Black Mesa
Dogie Mountain
UNITED STATES
Terlingua
(ghost town)
Study Butte
Big Bend
Travel Park
118
Maverick Mountain
9 miles
Villa de la Mina
To Presidio
Maverick
170
Rio Grande
Terlingua Creek
Lajitas
Lajitas Museum and Desert Garden
Burro Mesa
Pouroff Overlook
RATTLESNAKE
MOUNTAINS
MESA DE ANGUILA
14 miles
Luna's Jacal
MEXICO
Terlingua Abaja
Santa Elena
Canyon Overlook
SANTA ELENA
CANYON
Cerro Castellan
1004
3293
Mule Ears Peak
1193
3881
8 miles
Cottonwood
Castolon
661
2169
Santa
Elena
SIERRA DE SANTA ELENA
North
0 1 5 10 Kilometers
0 1 5 10 Miles
Unpaved road
Ranger station
Campground
Primitive road (four wheel drive, high clearance vehicles only)
Food and lodging
1143
3750
Elevations are shown in meters, with feet in italics.
Ruins
Private land within park boundary. Please observe land owners rights.
Mileage computation points

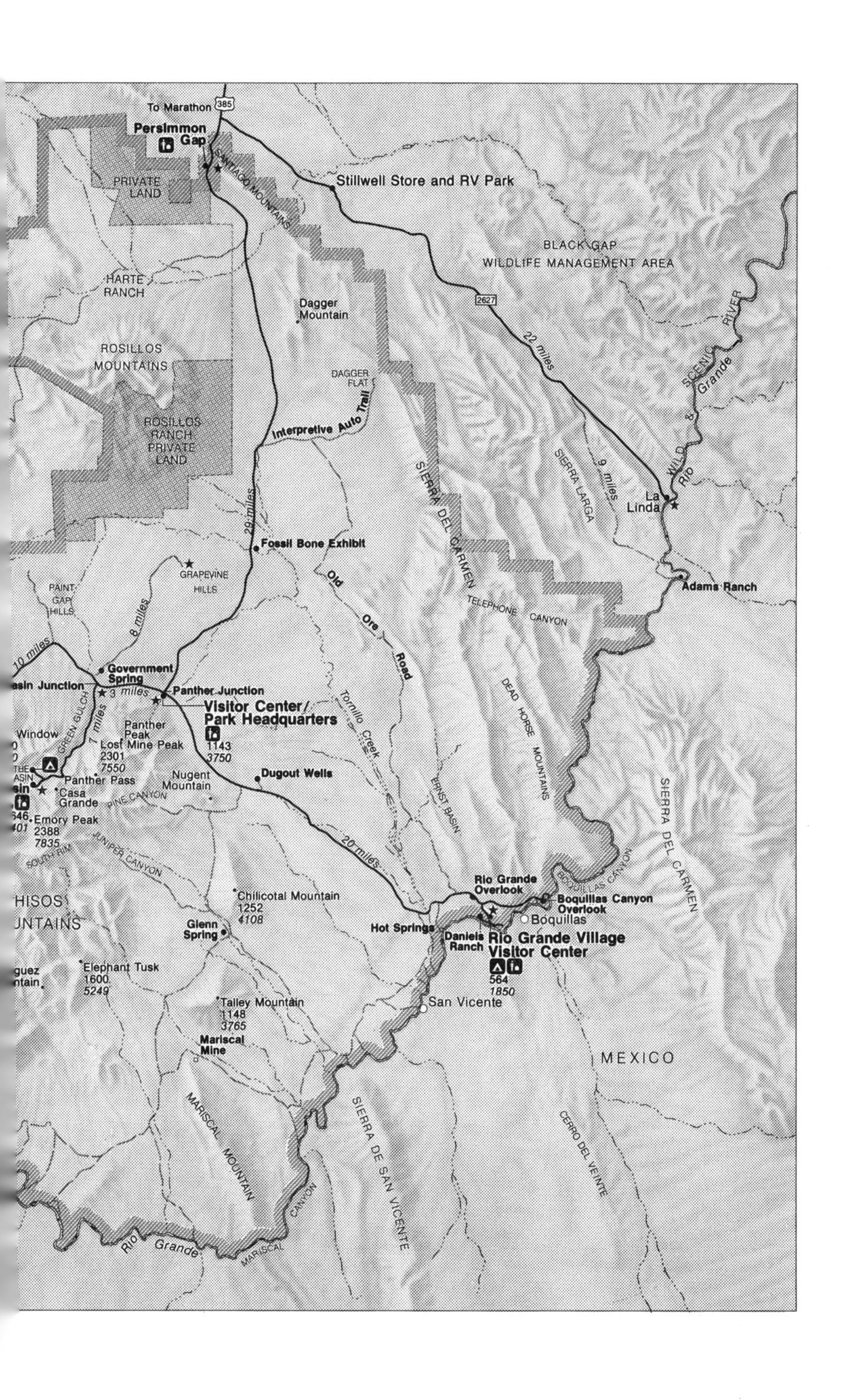
To Marathon
385
Persimmon Gap
SANTIAGO MOUNTAINS
PRIVATE LAND
Stillwell Store and RV Park
BLACK GAP
WILDLIFE MANAGEMENT AREA
HARTE RANCH
Dagger Mountain
2627
22 miles
ROSILLOS MOUNTAINS
DAGGER FLAT
ROSILLOS RANCH PRIVATE LAND
Interpretive Auto Trail
RIVER
SCENIC
Grande
WILD &
Rio
SIERRA DEL CARMEN
SIERRA LARGA
9 miles
La Linda
29 miles
Fossil Bone Exhibit
GRAPEVINE HILLS
Old Ore Road
Adams Ranch
PAINT GAP HILLS
8 miles
TELEPHONE CANYON
10 miles
Government Spring
Panther Junction
3 miles
Visitor Center/ Park Headquarters
1143
3750
GREEN GULCH
7 miles
Window
Panther Peak
Lost Mine Peak
2301
7550
Tornillo Creek
DEAD HORSE MOUNTAINS
Panther Pass
Nugent Mountain
Dugout Wells
Casa Grande
PINE CANYON
Emory Peak
2388
7835
ERNST BASIN
SIERRA DEL CARMEN
SOUTH RIM
JUNIPER CANYON
20 miles
Rio Grande Overlook
BOQUILLAS CANYON
Boquillas Canyon Overlook
Chilicotal Mountain
1252
4108
Boquillas
Hot Springs
Glenn Spring
Daniels Ranch
Rio Grande Village Visitor Center
564
1850
Elephant Tusk
1600
5249
Talley Mountain
1148
3765
San Vicente
Mariscal Mine
MEXICO
MARISCAL MOUNTAIN
SIERRA DE SAN VICENTE
CERRO DEL VEINTE
CANYON
Rio Grande
MARISCAL